DISCARD

I LOVE THAT MINIFIGURE

CONTENTS

Welcome to the wonderful world of LEGO® minifigures! You'll find hundreds of colorful characters in this book, on pages packed full of fascinating facts and trivia. They come from all eras, from 1978 to 2015, so what are you waiting for? Let's dive right in!

LET'S DO THIS!

HOW TO USE THIS BOOK

FIND OUT ABOUT ME ON PAGE 93!

I Love That Minifigure shows you some of the coolest, rarest, and most unusual minifigures ever produced by the LEGO Group. It is divided into 11 themed sections and each page is a mine of minifigure information.

Numbered annotations pick out the key features of each minifigure.

This is the name by which the character is most commonly known (many early minifigures did not have official names).

Quotes from LEGO designers give insights into the minifigure design process.

These boxes feature information about a related minifigure, or a variant of the main featured minifigure.

SAUSAGE SANDWICH BOARD!

HOT DOG GUY

ONE OF A KIND

I APPROACH MY JOB WITH RELISH!

1 Unique "sandwich board" piece shaped like a hot dog

2 Cheerful expression... Mmm, hot dogs!

3 Plain tan torso matches bun color

"The initial design didn't have any mustard, but the final version has just the right amount of zig-zag sauce!"
GITTE THORSEN, LEGO DESIGN MASTER

This box is your at-a-glance guide to each minifigure's place in LEGO history.

1 Not really rare, but still cool!

2 Not too difficult to find, with a bit of searching

3 Appears in only a small number of sets, or in blind polybags

4 Rare—you're lucky if you have this minifigure!

5 Very rare— a legendary minifigure!

There's never been a Minifigure quite like this character! His detailed hot dog outfit is all one piece and fits over the minifigure's head like any other headgear. Maybe he sells hot dogs, or perhaps he just really likes them!

HOT DOGS! GET YOUR HOT DOGS!
Released in 2013, the LEGO® Creator Hot Dog Stand (set 40078) was free to VIP members of LEGO.com with qualifying purchases. The set included a hot dog chef.

MINI STATS

Theme
LEGO® Minifigures

Year
2015

First appearance
LEGO Minifigures Series 13

Rarity
113

This is where you'll find out how rare each minifigure is—or isn't!

CHAPTER ONE
EVERYDAY HEROES

HERE'S TO THE DEDICATED MINIFIGURES WHO WORK TIRELESSLY TO BE THE MOST AWESOME THEY CAN BE!

I'M NUMBER ONE!

FIRST TRUE MINIFIGURE

1 All male minifigures wore hats until male hair pieces appeared in 1979

2 Very simply printed face, with dots for eyes and curved line for a smile

3 Torso decoration is a sticker, not printing

4 Badge identifies him as a member of the LEGO® police force

POLICEMAN

With posable arms and legs, and a printed face, this policeman is the first true minifigure. Before him, LEGO characters were mostly static figures with little playability. He is too big to fit into his police car, though, so he has to sit on its hood!

A NEW LOOK

LEGOLAND Town police officers have had several stylish looks over the years. In 1993, an update introduced a new police logo with a gold star on a black and white badge, and new head pieces with additional facial features.

Theme
LEGO® City

Year
2015

First appearance
Service Truck (60073)

Rarity

Where would LEGO City be without its construction workers? In a big mess, that's where! This minifigure is one of the latest recruits to the army of orange-suited workmen, but he only appears in one set, so catch him while you can.

UPDATED CLASSIC

CONSTRUCTION WORKER

1 Helmet with built-in ear defenders—new for 2015

2 No other construction worker has this face print

3 Unique torso design shows hooded top under work clothes

4 Gray hands represent gloves

FILM STAR
THE LEGO® MOVIE™ introduced us to the most famous construction worker of all: the lovable Emmet!

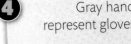

A PROUD TRADITION
LEGO construction workers date back to the earliest minifigure days, with the first seen in 1979. Construction sets returned in 2015 after a six-year absence.

The Diner Waitress has a real retro look, with her horn-rimmed specs and 1950s-style hair piece. What really makes her stand out, however, are her accessories—never before had a minifigure had such a cool set of wheels but no car!

HOW MAY I HELP YOU?
Diner Waitress is the only Series 11 Minifigure with a double-sided head piece. One side of her face has a wide smile, while the other has an annoyed frown.

**MINI STATS**

Theme
LEGO® Minifigures

Year
2013

First appearance
LEGO Minifigures Series 11

Rarity

DINER WAITRESS

NAMESAKE
The Diner Waitress is named "Tara", after Tara Wike: the LEGO designer she is based on!

1 Whipped ice cream-style hairdo

2 Double-sided head has two expressions

3 Ice cream sundae balanced on a white serving tray

4 Rockin' pink roller skates!

LEGO DESIGNER'S SECOND JOB!

FIRST PRINTED TORSO

TICKETS, PLEASE!

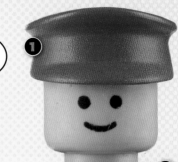

① Red cap first seen on 1975's non-posable LEGO® figures

② Blue torso with jacket and tie printing featured in more than 30 sets up to 2003

③ Posable leg design essentially unchanged after nearly 40 years

TRAIN CONDUCTOR

All aboard!

The train conductor is the first minifigure to have a printed torso. Previously, torsos had been stickered or left plain, but now designs were printed directly onto the torso piece.

AN ENDURING CHARACTER

Two years after the Train Conductor first appeared, a new Train Guard arrived on the scene. He wore the same hat, but had a different torso design and blue pants. He was included in more than a dozen sets over the course of the next six years.

MINI STATS

Theme
LEGOLAND® Town

Year
1978

First appearance
Car Transport Wagon (167)

Rarity

I'M CREATING A NEW ACRYLONITRILE BUTADIENE STYRENE MOLECULE!

SMART SET!

CHEMIST

1 Modern hairstyle piece has a ponytail at the back

2 Reversible head has a serious look on one side and a shocked expression on the other

3 Exclusive torso printing features pens and ID card

4 Lab coat print continued on back of the torso

MINI STATS

Theme
LEGO® Ideas

Year
2014

First appearance
Research Institute
(21110)

Rarity

Take a closer look at the world with one of the three exclusive scientists included in the Research Institute set. This was chosen to become a real LEGO set from hundreds of fan-built models submitted to the LEGO Ideas website.

REAL SCIENCE

The Chemist is based on Dr. Ellen Kooijman, the real-life geoscientist who came up with the idea for the Research Institute set.

LAB PARTNERS

The Chemist is joined in the Research Institute by a Paleontologist studying a huge dinosaur skeleton, and an Astronomer with a telescope.

MINI STATS

Theme
LEGO® Minifigures

Year
2011

First appearance
LEGO Minifigures
Series 4

Rarity

Hazmat Guy's job is to deal with hazardous materials, so it's understandable that he looks so anxious! Luckily, he is protected by his new and exclusive Hazmat helmet, with its built-in visor and radiation warning symbol.

DANGEROUS WORK

Hazmat Guy is not the only one with a dangerous job. The Dino Tracker from Minifigures Series 13 seems to enjoy hers, though!

HAZMAT GUY

HOW WILL I EAT MY LUNCH IN THIS SUIT?

1 Unique helmet with clear visor

2 Anxious face with printed stress lines!

3 Hazard icon printed on helmet bib, and on torso beneath

4 Spray gun with hose fits on to back of helmet

CAMEO

The Robo SWATS in THE LEGO® MOVIE™ wear Hazmat suits, too.

UNIQUE HELMET

Theme
LEGOLAND® Town

Year
1978

First appearance
Ambulance (606)

Rarity

The first-ever female minifigure works as a nurse aboard the LEGOLAND Town Ambulance. Released in 1978, she is also the only medic minifigure to have a sticker on her torso, instead of printed details.

FIRST FEMALE

NO ROOM
The nurse's ambulance is too small for her to fit inside, but she can ride on the hood or the roof.

NURSE

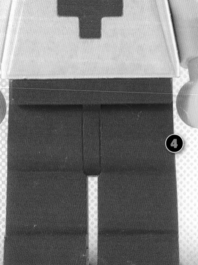

AT LAST! WITH LEGS, I CAN FINALLY SIT DOWN!

1 Same hair piece worn by non-posable LEGO® figures from 1975

2 Head piece has the original simple face printing on it

3 Plain white torso with red cross sticker

4 Posable legs—still a novelty in 1978!

WELL EQUIPPED

In 1980, a variant of this medical minifigure appeared in Paramedic Unit (set 6364). Her torso is printed with details including a stethoscope and a pocket with a pen.

BASEBALL PLAYER

COVERS ALL THE BASES!

TAKE ME OUT TO THE BALL GAME!

1 New hat mold has since been worn by the Rapper, Lumberjack, and Baseball Fielder Minifigures

2 Baseball bat also carried by Nelson Muntz from LEGO® The Simpsons™

3 "Clutchers" team name refers to the "clutch power" that holds LEGO bricks together

4 Plain white legs are unique, thanks to belt printing on hips

This sporting hero was the first to wield a LEGO baseball bat, but he is not the first LEGO baseball player. In 1999, a special Boston Red Sox minifigure was given away at the team's Fenway Park stadium. He also wore a red cap and a white uniform, and is now very rare indeed!

PERFECT CATCH

In 2013, a Baseball Fielder with a "Stackers" uniform and a catcher's mitt instead of a left hand featured as part of Minifigures series 10.

MINI STATS

Theme
LEGO® Minifigures

Year
2011

First appearance
LEGO Minifigures Series 3

Rarity

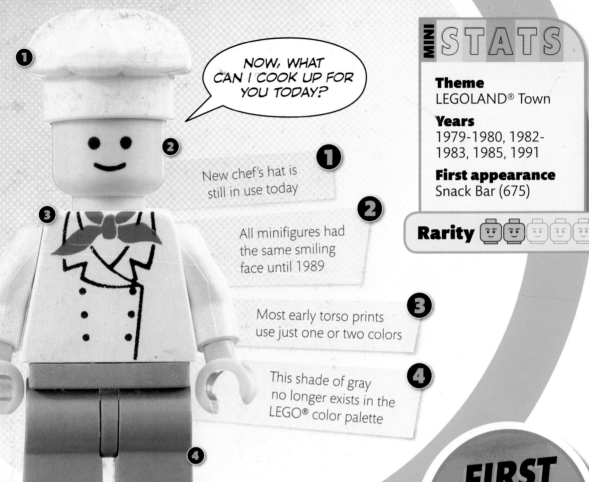

NOW, WHAT CAN I COOK UP FOR YOU TODAY?

Theme
LEGOLAND® Town

Years
1979-1980, 1982-1983, 1985, 1991

First appearance
Snack Bar (675)

Rarity

1 New chef's hat is still in use today

2 All minifigures had the same smiling face until 1989

3 Most early torso prints use just one or two colors

4 This shade of gray no longer exists in the LEGO® color palette

CHEF

FIRST CHEF'S HAT!

PIZZA THE ACTION

Behind door 21 of the 2005 LEGO® City Advent Calendar (set 7324) is a Pizza Chef minifigure. Wearing the iconic chef's hat, he's ready to serve some tasty pizza. But from the look of his tubby tummy print, he eats almost as much food as he serves!

In 1979, LEGOLAND Town got its very first snack bar. Now hungry minifigures could fill their bellies with the many delicious treats cooked by the hard-working Chef. This Chef's special offering is his hat— he is the first minifigure to wear one like it!

MINI STATS

Theme
LEGO® Racers

Year
2009

First appearance
Ferrari Victory
(8168)

Rarity

A rare example of a real person becoming a minifigure, Brazilian racing driver Felipe Massa first appeared in LEGO form in 2007 in a yellow helmet. This blue-helmeted variant appeared in just one set in 2009.

REAL-WORLD RACER

RED ALL OVER
The 2015 LEGO® Speed Champions theme features all new Ferrari vehicles and drivers.

FELIPE MASSA

I CAN'T WAIT TO GET OUT ON THE TRACK!

1 Same face print also used for Rubens Barrichello minifigure

2 A stickered torso is a rarity on modern minifigures

3 Sticker includes Ferrari logo and Brazilian flag

4 Ferrari-red legs and torso

REAL RACERS

Massa isn't the only Ferrari racing driver to appear as a minifigure: Rubens Barrichello and Kimi Räikkönen are among the other racers to have had this honor.

Theme
LEGOLAND® Town

Years
1982-1983, 1985, 1991

First appearance
Post Office (6362)

Rarity

LEGOLAND Town got its first delivery service in 1982 with the Post Office and Mail Truck sets. Both featured this jolly Postman, who has a red torso printed with the bugle-shaped post office logo on the left-hand side, and matching black hat and legs.

FIRST MAIL MINIFIG

POSTMAN

I'M SURE TO GET LOTS OF FAN MAIL!

1 Another postal worker and a Fire Captain also wore this new black hat in 1982

2 The LEGO® post office logo is a bugle or post horn.

3 Black is the most common color for minifigure legs, appearing in more than 950 sets!

MODERN MAIL

In 2008, the LEGO City postal service zoomed into the modern world with Air Mail (set 7732), part of the Cargo subtheme. The set includes an Air Mail Worker wearing cool sunglasses and a cap.

FULLY BOOKED!

> I'VE ALWAYS WANTED TO BE IN A BOOK!

LIBRARIAN

TITULAR TITTERS

The title *Oranges and Peaches* is a joke mishearing of *On the Origin of Species* by Charles Darwin.

1 Hair mold first seen on Ginny Weasley from Harry Potter theme

2 Mug has a message for noisy visitors to the library

3 Book accessory can be opened and closed

Oranges and Peaches

This bespectacled bookworm features all-unique printing, including the "Shhh!" on her coffee mug! Part of the range of collectible Minifigures launched in 2010, she has her own online bio that describes her love for books of all kinds—including ones about minifigures, no doubt!

JUST A THEORY

Could the Librarian be based on Amy from the TV comedy *The Big Bang Theory*? The show was made into a LEGO set in 2015 as part of the LEGO® Ideas theme.

MINI STATS

Theme
LEGO® Minifigures

Year
2013

First appearance
LEGO Minifigures Series 10

Rarity

HEY, WHERE'D THE BALL GO?

1

2

3

RARE SOCCER STAR

BRAZIL-IANT!
The 2002 FIFA World Cup was won by Brazil.

1 Rare face print with mustache

2 Number 59 printed on back of torso

3 The Coca-Cola logo was invented in 1886!

This soccer player is one of two special minifigures that were available as part of a Coca-Cola promotion celebrating the 2002 FIFA World Cup. The LEGO Group released a range of other soccer-themed sets in the same year.

MINI STATS

Theme
LEGO® Sports

Year
2002

First appearance
Secret Set A (4471)

Rarity

STRIKING IN SILVER
Secret Set B (set 4472), released at the same time as Set A, featured a player in a silver strip with a brown hair piece. He also has the number 59 on his back.

MINI STATS

Theme
LEGO® Minifigures

Year
2012

First appearance
LEGO Minifigures
Series 6

Rarity

The Surgeon Minifigure comes with a brand new scrubs cap piece and is unusual because you cannot see her mouth beneath her printed mask. However, her friendly eyes suggest there is a traditional LEGO smile underneath it, ready to reassure her patients.

MEDIC IN A MASK

SURGEON

THIS WON'T HURT A BIT!

1 Exclusive scrubs cap

2 White hands look like surgical gloves

3 Syringe piece also used by Nurse from Minifigures Series 1

4 X-ray piece has the same proportions as a LEGO Skeleton figure

SCREEN SURGEON

A similar female surgeon is among the Master Builders in THE LEGO® MOVIE™.

MEET DR MCSCRUBS!

THE LEGO MOVIE features a male surgeon character in the form of Dr. McScrubs. He can be seen when the citizens of Bricksburg learn how to be Master Builders.

This exclusive soccer goalkeeper was part of a promotional set given out with some pairs of Adidas sneakers in 2007. He came with a gold and silver soccer ball, "glove" hands, and a display stand. The name "Stripes" is printed on the back of his torso.

THIS ONE'S A KEEPER!

MINI STATS

Theme
LEGO® Sports

Year
2007

First appearance
Superstar Figure (3573)

Rarity

ADIDAS SUPER GOALIE

SCORE PAST ME IF YOU CAN!

1 Spiky hair piece is made from rubber

2 "Stripes" and "3" printed on back— but no stripes!

3 A variant Stripes has the Adidas logo printed on the front of his torso.

4 Hands can hold oversized "goalie" gloves

SAFE HANDS
Stripes' gloves have a real LEGO rarity: fingers and thumbs!

HERO HAIR
Super Goalie has the same stylish hair as the LEGO® DC Comics™ Super Heroes minifigure Nightwing!

SHE DIGS BONES!

PALEONTOLOGIST

1 — Helmet and hair are one piece

2 — Two-tone printed arms look like short sleeves

3 — New ammonite fossil accessory

4 — Unique leg piece printed with shorts, socks, and boots

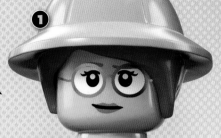

"My favorite part of this minifigure is the helmet designed by my colleague Gitte Thorsen—it's awesome!"
CHRIS B. JOHANSEN, LEGO DESIGN MASTER

Dressed in safari gear, the Paleontologist is on a mission to dig up some dinosaurs! She's made a good start with her bone and brand new fossil piece. Let's hope she shares her discoveries with her fellow paleontologist from 2014's Research Institute set!

DEM BONES, DEM BONES!

The Paleontologist's bone first appeared in 2011 and since then has featured in more than 50 different sets, including the Cave Woman from Minifigures Series 5.

MINI STATS

Theme
LEGO® Minifigures

Year
2015

First appearance
LEGO Minifigures Series 13

Rarity

CHRIS PRATT'S BACK!

THAT'S AN AWESOME DINOSAUR!

1 Same face and hair as Star-Lord from LEGO® Marvel Super Heroes

2 Flesh tones are used only for licensed themes, such as movie-based sets

3 Unique torso print

OWEN GRADY

Owen Grady is an ordinary researcher in an extraordinary place: he gets to work with dinosaurs at the Jurassic World theme park. It sounds like a dream job, until things go wrong and he finds himself in the middle of a Raptor Rampage! He is part of the new Jurassic World theme, based on the movie of the same name.

22

MINI STATS

Theme
LEGO® Jurassic World™

Year
2015

First appearance
Raptor Rampage (75917)

Rarity

DON'T I KNOW YOU?

Owen is actor Chris Pratt's third brush with the world of LEGO minifigures. He was the voice of Emmet in THE LEGO® MOVIE™ and his *Guardians of the Galaxy* movie character, Star-Lord, has also been made into a minifigure.

CHAPTER TWO
YOU'RE HISTORY!

TRAVEL BACK
IN TIME TO SEE
HOW MINIFIGURES
HAVE PLAYED THEIR
PART ALL THROUGH
THE HISTORY OF
THE WORLD!

1 Helmet color is unique to this minifigure

2 Torso print is a cuirass— a muscly piece of armor

3 Spear also carried by the Tribal Chief from Minifigures Series 3

4 Crimson fabric cape

MINIFIGURES, PREPARE FOR GLORY!

SPARTAN

MINI STATS

Theme
LEGO® Minifigures

Year
2010

First appearance
LEGO Minifigures
Series 2

Rarity

A brave and fearsome warrior, the Spartan features all-unique printing, right down to his sandals! He carries a new, rubber-tipped spear and a shield that can be decorated with other LEGO pieces.

GREEK AND UNIQUE!

HISTORICAL HEADGEAR
The Spartan's distinctive helmet is the same as the one seen on the Temple Statue in the LEGO® Atlantis theme, only in bronze.

MINI STATS

Theme
LEGO® Pirates

Years
1989, 1991, 1993, 1995–1997, 2001–2002

First appearance
Forbidden Island (6270)

Rarity

In 1989, LEGO Pirates introduced the very first minifigures with different faces and body parts. Captain Redbeard has a peg-leg, a hook for a hand, a printed eyepatch, and a beard. After him, minifigures were never the same!

FIRST OF A NEW BREED!

CAPTAIN REDBEARD

WALK THE PLANK!

1 Only this variant of Redbeard has printing on his hat

2 No minifigure had ever had facial hair or an eyepatch before!

3 New epaulet element over unique torso

4 Hook functions just as well as a regular minifigure hand

COMIC CAPERS

A LEGO Pirates comic book, *The Golden Medallion*, was released in 1989.

CAPTAIN BRICKBEARD

In 2009, a new captain commanded the pirates. Brickbeard also has an eyepatch, hook-hand, and peg-leg. Could he be Captain Redbeard reborn?

The glitzy Gold Knight is a hero from the Fantasy Era of the LEGO Castle theme. He must have used magic to strengthen his armor and weapons, as gold is normally a soft metal—good for decoration but not for fighting!

KNIGHT SHINING BRIGHT!

MINI STATS

Theme
LEGO® Castle

Year
2009

First appearance
Drawbridge Defense (7079)

Rarity

GOLD KNIGHT

I'M FROM THE GOLDEN AGE!

SKELETON CREW

Drawbridge Defense also included three spooky foes for the Gold Knight to battle: a white skeleton, a black skeleton, and a scythe-wielding skeleton riding —you guessed it—a skeleton horse!

1 Dark gray hair and mustache

2 Gold chrome sword

3 Unique breastplate

A HEAD-DRESS TO IMPRESS!

I CAN'T REALLY SEE IN THIS THING!

1 Headdress can be held by minifigure hands

2 Stern face is printed with two gray stripes

3 Back of cape depicts stylized minifigure head

4 Unique printing continues on legs

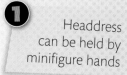

ACHU

CAPTIVATING CAPES

The first fabric cape on a minifigure was introduced in 1993 for the LEGOLAND® Castle Red Dragon Master. The cape showed a green fire-breathing dragon with red wings.

MINI STATS

Theme
LEGO® Adventurers

Year
1999

First appearance
Ruler of the Jungle (5906)

Rarity

In the heart of the jungle, this minifigure guards an ancient treasure called the sundisc—and he's not about to give it up! Every part of Achu is unique, including his spectacular bird-themed headdress, and his torso printing complete with belly button!

27

HISS!

1 New printed hair piece

2 Torso print shows elaborate hawk and winged snake jewelry

3 Green snake seen in several LEGO® NINJAGO™ sets

4 White slope piece with ornate printed detail

EGYPTIAN QUEEN

ROYAL RELATION

The appearance of the Egyptian Queen was inspired by that of Queen Cleopatra VII, the last pharaoh of Egypt.

MINI STATS

Theme
LEGO® Minifigures

Year
2011

First appearance
LEGO Minifigures
Series 5

Rarity

This regal Minifigure boasts a brand new hair piece, printed with a winged scarab. The rest of her printing is also new and exclusive to her. To give the impression of a dress, she has a sloped piece in place of standard minifigure legs.

A PAIR OF PHARAOHS

The first Ancient Egypt-inspired character in the Minifigures theme was the Pharaoh from Series 2. Could he rule alongside the Egyptian Queen?

MINI STATS

Theme
THE LEGO® MOVIE™

Year
2014

First appearance
LEGO Minifigures
The LEGO MOVIE
Series

Rarity

When you blast through a portal into a new realm, it's important to get a disguise. This variant of THE LEGO MOVIE's Wyldstyle wears a floor-length dress and wouldn't look out of place in any Old West saloon—nor in a collection of well-dressed minifigures!

OLD-TIMEY DISGUISE!

WYLDSTYLE (WILD WEST)

1 Only one variant of Wyldstyle (in a hood) doesn't wear this hair

2 Exclusive face, torso, and skirt printing

3 Kimono Girl from Minifigures Series 4 also carries this fan, but in red

4 This is the only variant of Wyldstyle to have a slope piece instead of legs

"I worked on the early phase of THE LEGO MOVIE when the characters were still not totally defined. This outfit was originally designed for a robot lady in a Western saloon, and it was red."
ALEXANDRE BOUDON,
LEGO DESIGN MASTER

The Forestman began life as the leader of six outlaws guarding a treasure chest in a forest hideout. His companions wore blue, black, or red feathers in their caps, and had matching arms and printed collars. All six looked like merry men!

FIRST TO WEAR GREEN

MINI STATS

Theme
LEGOLAND® Castle

Years
1987–1988

First appearance
Camouflaged Outpost (6066)

Rarity

FORESTMAN

1. Feathers of different colors and sizes can be added to this new hat

2. Quiver of arrows fits between head and torso

3. The Forestmen were the first minifigures to wear green

4. Money pouch on waistband

YOU MAY BE OLDER SIR, BUT WHERE IS YOUR MUSTACHE?

REDESIGNED ROGUE

A more detailed Forestman with a goatee beard, thin mustache, and cheeky smile was included in the first series of LEGO® Minifigures in 2010.

UNIQUE MAJESTIC MASK

YOU'D LOOK SURPRISED IN THIS, TOO!

1 Detachable white plume

2 White painted face with red stripes under mask

3 Printed necklace of pearls and animal teeth

4 Grass skirt on "bare" legs

KING KAHUKA

LEGO Pirates have to be careful where they bury their treasure, as they run the risk of bumping into King Kahuka and his tribe of island warriors! The King and his unique mask feature in six LEGO Pirates sets.

UNMASKED!

A variant Kahuka, with hair and no mask, appears in Forbidden Cove (set 6264).

MINI STATS

Theme
LEGO® Pirates

Years
1994, 1995, 2001

First appearance
King Kahuka (6236)

Rarity

MEET THE NATIVES

Kahuka's tribe wield bows and spears, and have black hair pieces with white feathers or animal horns in them. Male islanders have brightly painted faces, while females have the classic female head piece of the era.

KNIGHT KNIGHT!

RARE CASTLE HERO

TOURNAMENT KNIGHT

1 Visor clips onto helmet and can swivel up and down

2 Helmet is shared with the classic red spaceman

3 Printed shield emblem

4 Black legs with red hips seen on over 100 minifigures

FIVE KNIGHTS
This knight's torso design was used on just five other minifigures.

This brave knight is one of a matching pair released with two knights from a rival faction, who wore different helmets, colors, and torso designs. The set also included a sword, an ax, a hatchet, and a shield.

FRIGHT KNIGHTS
The terrifying Fright Knights appeared in 1997, ruled not by a king but by the dreaded Basil the Bat Lord—who rode a black dragon called Draco!

MINI STATS

Theme
LEGO® Castle

Year
1983

First appearance
Castle Figures
(6002)

Rarity

MINI STATS

Theme
LEGO® Vikings

Year
2006

First appearance
Vikings Chess Set
(G577)

Rarity

The LEGO Vikings Chess Set was released in 2006, alongside two other Vikings sets. To avoid getting the minifigures mixed up, which would make it hard to use them as chess pieces, some of their elements were glued together. In the set, the Red King and his army went into battle against a matching team in blue.

VIKING CHESS PIECE!

RED KING

THIS IS NO GAME!

1 Horns are glued to helmet

2 Red fabric cape also worn by Red Queen

3 He wields a golden sword on the chessboard

DWARFED
The Viking chess pieces have the same torso design as the dwarves in 2008 Castle sets.

Peabody Public Library
Columbia City, IN

SAVAGE WARRIOR
The Barbarian Armor Viking was one of the first Norse fighters released in 2005. His ragged armor and raging expression mark him out as a warrior to be avoided on the battlefield!

The **Forestwoman is** a reissue of a character from Forestmen's Crossing (set 6071), which was originally released in 1990 as part of the LEGO® Castle theme. Twenty years later she returned in Volume 5 of the Vintage Minifigures series, only this time without her quiver of arrows. Her printed torso piece features a tight green corset and necklace, and her face retains the red lips and printed hair of the original.

MINI **STATS**

Theme
LEGO® Classic

Year
2010

First appearance
LEGO Vintage Minifigures Vol. 5 (852769)

Rarity

FORESTWOMAN

I'M SO GOOD THEY MADE ME TWICE!

GIRL POWER!

Volume 5 of the Vintage Minifigure Collection was an all-female set, featuring a Doctor, an Air Steward, a Ninja, a woman with a red jacket, and the Forestwoman.

❶ Green hat also seen in LEGO® Pirates theme

❷ Hair printed on head piece

❸ This was the only female minifigure face print until 1992

BUSY CROSSING

Forestmen's Crossing includes four different forestmen, but only the Forestwoman is found in no other LEGO Castle sets.

RARE VINTAGE REPLICA

FOUR SCORE AND SEVEN BRICKS AGO...

ABRAHAM LINCOLN

1 Combined hat-and-beard piece created just for this Minifigure

2 Face printing shows off Lincoln's distinctive jawline

3 Lines from the Gettysburg Address printed on tile piece

FIRST PRESIDENT MINIFIGURE

Honest Abe has an exclusive element that combines his trademark hat and beard in one piece. His inclusion along with William Shakespeare in THE LEGO MOVIE theme marks the first time that real historical figures have been made into minifigures.

WILL WITH A QUILL

Like Abraham Lincoln, the William Shakespeare Minifigure has a tile that looks like a paper manuscript, but his reads: "To build... or not to build". He also carries a quill pen.

MINI STATS

Theme
THE LEGO® MOVIE™

Year
2014

First appearance
LEGO Minifigures
The LEGO MOVIE
Series

Rarity

35

1

MY HAT CAN STOP TRAFFIC!

1 Cone-shaped "henin" hat

2 Printed female face first seen in LEGO® Pirates sets in 1989

3 Sloped skirt piece instead of legs

PRINTS CHARMING

The Forestwoman has the same torso print as the Maiden, but in green instead of blue.

FIRST DRESS!

MAIDEN

MINI STATS

Theme
LEGO® Castle

Year
1990

First appearance
King's Mountain Fortress (6081)

Rarity

This fair Maiden has the first non-standard face on a LEGO Castle minifigure, with printed hair and red lips instead of the classic eyes and smile. She also had a sloped piece instead of legs—the first time a minifigure had worn a skirt!

OLD MAIDEN

An earlier Maiden featured in Guarded Inn (set 6067) from 1986. She wears the same hat, but has a standard minifigure face and legs, and a simpler torso design.

MINI STATS

Theme
LEGO® Adventurers

Years
1998–1999

First appearance
Adventurers Tomb (2996)

Rarity

LEGO Adventurers was a new theme for 1998, centered on the search for the Re-Gou Ruby in Egypt. Pharaoh Hotep was the creepy king who guarded the ruby, and the first ever LEGO mummy! He has unique head, leg, and torso printing.

ARE YOU MY MUMMY?

OH MUMMY!
The word "mummy" comes from the ancient Persian word for an embalmed body. Yuck!

PHARAOH HOTEP

1 Ancient Egyptian headdresses such as these are known as "nemes"

2 Rare minifigure nostrils!

3 Blue segmented body armor

4 Toe print on leg piece

THAT WRAPS IT UP!

The LEGO® Studios theme got in on the mummy action in 2002 with Curse Of The Pharaoh (set 1383). Its mummy has a bandaged head, torso, and legs, and a less colorful take on Pharaoh Hotep's headdress.

37

This dashing knight could only be found in the Black Knight's Castle set, along with three other knights wearing plumes of red, blue, and yellow respectively. All four knights had their own lance, sword, and tapering kite-shaped shield, decorated with a multicolored dragon design.

BEAUTIFUL PLUMAGE!

MINI STATS

Theme
LEGO® Castle

Year
1992

First appearance
Black Knight's Castle
(6086)

Rarity

WHITE PLUME KNIGHT

JOUST A MINUTE!

1 Elegant, dragon-shaped plume

2 Plumes on both sides of helmet

3 Pointed visor moves up and down

4 Breastplate armor piece over blue torso with printed armor

EVIL EYES

This cross-looking Evil Knight with a kite-shaped shield was included as part of LEGO® Minifigures Series 7 in 2012. Shame he's not wearing a visor to hide that face!

ANOTHER KIND OF NINJA!

FEMALE NINJA

I'M GREEN AND RARELY SEEN!

1 Head printed with long eyelashes and a headband

2 A clip on the back of the head wrap can hold a katana sword

3 Shuriken and dagger hidden in printed robe

1

2

3

MIRROR NINJA
The green Male Ninja wears his dagger and shuriken (throwing star) the other way round from the Female Ninja.

One of the first female characters to appear in the LEGO Castle Ninja subtheme, this well-armed warrior came in a three-minifigure set with a green Male Ninja and a Samurai Lord. Each came with a display base that also held a collector's card.

EVERYTHING'S GONE GREEN
In LEGO® NINJAGO™, Lloyd Garmadon becomes the legendary Green Ninja, destined to win the great battle between good and evil—if he can master the art of Spinjitzu first!

MINI STATS

Theme
LEGO® Castle

Year
2000

First appearance
Mini Heroes Collection
Ninja #3 (3346)

Rarity

ONE MUST FIGHT WITH HONOR!

1 Horn piece serves as crest on helmet

2 Printed hair frames face

3 Kendo armor also used in LEGO® NINJAGO™ sets

4 Antique pistol element introduced in 1989

SHOGUN

HIDDEN WEAPON

The Shogun's armor hides a dagger printed on his torso!

From his fierce expression, it's clear that this Shogun—also known as the Red Warlord—is not the sort of minifigure to be messed with. No wonder he comes in a set all by himself, with only a collector's card and a display stand for company!

MINI STATS

Theme
LEGO® Castle

Year
2000

First appearance
Mini Heroes Collection Ninja #1 (3344)

Rarity

SAMURAI'S BACK

LEGO® Minifigures Series 13 includes a tough-looking Samurai in a dark red update of the Shogun's armor. With a katana in each hand, will she fight with him or against him?

MINI STATS

Theme
LEGO® Minifigures

Year
2013

First appearance
LEGO Minifigures
Series 11

Rarity

With his mask, chain, and grass skirt, this scary-looking warrior has more than a little in common with King Kahuka from LEGO® Pirates. Both have smiling faces behind their masks, but only the Island Warrior has hair— as his mask is not worn on the top of his head.

COOL TRIBAL MASK

ISLAND WARRIOR

MM-GFMPH!

1 Tribal mask attached to torso via a neck bracket

2 Grinning face behind mask is printed with blue tattoos

3 Leg and torso printing echoes that of King Kahuka minifigure

4 Spear features in more than 200 sets

"I designed his tattoos to be covered by the mask. That way you get two characters in one."
CHRIS B. JOHANSEN, LEGO DESIGN MASTER

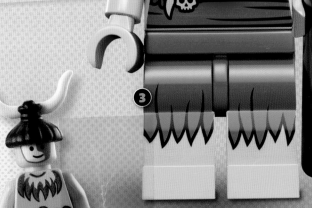

TRIBAL FASHION

Behind his mask, the Island Warrior has a black hair piece with a bone clipped in the top. The Islanders from LEGO® Pirates wore a similar style with horns or plumes.

One of a new, more detailed kind of minfigure introduced for the new LEGO Pirates theme in 1989, this Female Pirate is one of the first minifigures to have gender-specific printed details. A variant with a red bandana set sail in later playsets.

FIRST FEMALE FACE!

MINI STATS

Theme
LEGO® Pirates

Years
1989, 1993, 2002

First appaerance
Black Seas Barracuda (6285)

Rarity

CALL ME BANNED ANNA!

FEMALE PIRATE

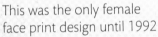

1 Bandana element was new for 1989

2 This was the only female face print design until 1992

3 First ever torso print to be specifically female

4 Plain legs—printing on this element was not introduced until 1994

FIRST LADIES

Ten years before the LEGO Pirates theme launched, LEGOLAND® Castle introduced one of the very first female minifigures: 1979's Princess.

SET SAIL

This pirate sailed on two ships: the *Black Seas Barracuda* and the *Skull's Eye Schooner* (set 6286).

CHAPTER THREE
OUT OF THIS WORLD

THERE HAVE BEEN MINIFIGURES EXPLORING SPACE SINCE 1978. CHECK OUT THIS COSMIC COLLECTION OF CLASSICS!

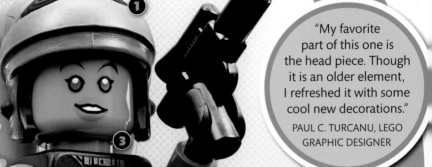

1 Head piece with uniquely printed lekku and goggles

2 Rare lime-green skin

3 Double-sided face print, with closed mouth on other side

4 Legs printed with rebel pilot uniform details

DON'T MESS WITH THE REBELS!

HERA SYNDULLA

RARE REBEL

OOLA'S THAT GIRL

Like Hera Syndulla, Oola is a green-skinned Twi'lek. She appears in Jabba's Palace (set 9516) and is made from all lime green elements, apart from her hips.

Hera Syndulla is a major character in the *Star Wars Rebels*™ animated series. Her minifigure has unusual lekku—or head-tails—that look as if they grow out of her head through her helmet. In fact, the helmet and the head-tails are all one molded piece.

MINI STATS

Theme
LEGO® Star Wars®

Year
2010

First appearance
Toys "R" Us
promotional giveaway

Rarity

A limited edition of 10,000, this silver chrome-painted stormtrooper minifigure was given away with LEGO *Star Wars* purchases from Toys "R" Us in 2010. There have been several stormtrooper variants over the years, but none shines as brightly as this one!

TROOP THE SILVER!

STORMTROOPER (CHROME)

HALT! I ORDER YOU TO ADMIRE ME!

1 Helmet and torso printed over silver chrome paint

2 Black head piece with no printing underneath helmet

3 Torso print used for all LEGO stormtroopers until a 2012 redesign

4 Black hands are not chrome-painted and can hold a blaster

IN THE SHADOWS

Featured in 2015's Shadow Troopers (set 75079), the matte-gray finish on the shadow trooper minifigure was inspired by the F-35 stealth fighter jet. The front of the helmet is a lighter shade for a skull-like look.

This minifigure is one of two included in the Exo Suit, which was the seventh fan proposal to get an official release as part of the LEGO Ideas project. Pete is named after Peter Reid, the LEGO fan and builder who originally created the set. He is based on the look of the classic LEGO® Space minifigures from the 1970s and '80s, but in a color that was never used at the time—green!

MINI **STATS**

Theme
LEGO® Ideas

Year
2014

First appearance
Exo Suit (21109)

Rarity

PETE

HE'S A SPACE FAN!

EXO-LLENT!

1 Helmet with clear visor is more robust than original LEGO Space helmets

2 Pete's head printing is the same as Zane's from LEGO® NINJAGO™

3 Green oxygen tank is exclusive to Exo Suit

4 Classic LEGO Space logo first seen in 1978

SPACE FOR ONE MORE

Pete is joined on his space adventure by Yve. Named after Peter Reid's girlfriend and fellow fan builder Yvonne Doyle, she wears the same spacesuit as Pete, but has a smiling, female face.

BIG PINK BRAIN!

THIS GALAXY IS MINE!

ALIEN VILLAINESS

1 Transparent pink brain is integral to green head piece

2 Chunky alien ray gun

3 Eyebrows, eyes, and lips printed on head piece

4 Printed slope piece instead of who knows how many legs!

Don't mess with the Alien Villainess! She's dressed to chill in her black and pink dress, and lilac cape—which, unlike most LEGO capes, is made from two separate parts. Her alien head also has a pink brain, rather than the more "usual" green kind.

ALIEN INVASION

The Alien Villainess looks remarkably similar to the Alien Commander from the LEGO® Alien Conquest play theme. Perhaps they intend to conquer the galaxy together?

MINI STATS

Theme
LEGO® Minifigures

Year
2012

First appearance
LEGO Minifigures Series 8

Rarity

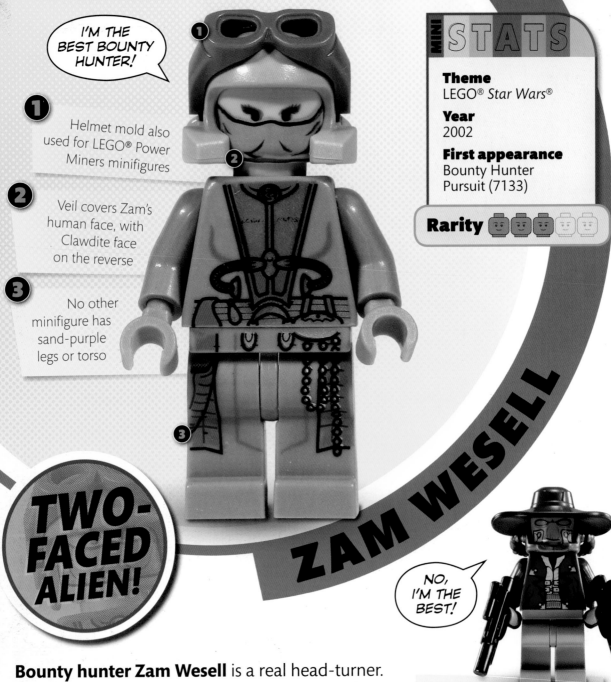

I'M THE BEST BOUNTY HUNTER!

1. Helmet mold also used for LEGO® Power Miners minifigures

2. Veil covers Zam's human face, with Clawdite face on the reverse

3. No other minifigure has sand-purple legs or torso

MINI STATS

Theme
LEGO® Star Wars®

Year
2002

First appearance
Bounty Hunter Pursuit (7133)

Rarity

TWO-FACED ALIEN!

ZAM WESELL

NO, I'M THE BEST!

Bounty hunter **Zam Wesell** is a real head-turner. Being a Clawdite shapeshifter, she can mimic the appearance of any species, and this minifigure's reversible head piece shows her human form on one side and her natural reptilian Clawdite form on the other. Appearing exclusively in Bounty Hunter Pursuit, finding this minifigure can be almost as hard as seeing the real Zam!

JEDI'S BANE

Like Zam Wesell, Cad Bane is also a bounty hunter. His minifigure features a wide-brimmed hat and detachable breathing apparatus, both of which are exclusive to him.

MINI STATS

Theme
LEGO® Star Wars®

Year
2003

First appearance
Cloud City (10123)

Rarity

This very rare variant of the galaxy's best bounty hunter is one of several minifigures exclusive to the rare Cloud City set from 2003. It is the second variant of Boba, and differs from the original only in its printed arms and legs.

RARE PRINTED ARMS

IN THE CLOUDS

Cloud City also boasts exclusive variants of Lando, Leia, and Luke.

BOBA FETT (CLOUD CITY)

GUYS... I'M RIGHT HERE!

1 Helmet has built-in jetpack behind

2 Plain black head piece shows through T-shaped slot in helmet

3 This is the very first minifigure to have printing on the arms

4 The first Boba from 2000 had plain gray arms and legs

YOUNG BOBA

A child version of Boba Fett comes with Jango Fett's *Slave I* (set 7153) from 2002. He has short blue legs and a yellow face.

49

Theme
LEGO® Space

Years
1993–1994

First appearance
Celestial Sled (6834)

Rarity

Befitting his status as leader of a team of hot-shot civilian scientists, this mustachioed minifigure has a unique torso with a formal jacket print. His orange visor was new to the LEGO Space Ice Planet 2002 subtheme and protects the Chief's distinctive white whiskers from the cold.

HAIR WEAR

The Chief isn't the only Ice Planet character with distinctive hair. Ice Planet Woman has fiery red locks, while Ice Planet Man sports blond bangs.

ICE PLANET CHIEF

> A FROZEN MUSTACHE IS NO LAUGHING MATTER!

1 New visor design has built-in antenna

2 Face print could show white hair or a layer of ice!

3 Standard breathing apparatus has not changed since 1978!

4 Small Ice Planet logo on torso

ICE DRIVE

The Ice Planet Chief features in two circuits of the LEGO *Racers* video game.

STONE COLD CLASSIC!

LEGO LEKKU!

IT'S LUCKY I LOOK GOOD IN STRIPES!

SHAAK TI

1 Blue printing continues on back of horns and on wide third lekku at back

2 Large eyes reflect style of *The Clone Wars* animated TV series

3 Face print joins up with head-piece design

TI TIME
Six years before the Shaak Ti minifigure was made, the character featured in LEGO *Star Wars: The Video Game.*

MINI STATS

Theme
LEGO® *Star Wars®*

Year
2011

First appearance
T-6 Jedi Shuttle (7931)

Rarity

Togruta Jedi Master Shaak Ti's most striking feature is her spectacular head-tails, or "lekku." Shaak Ti has three lekku: one running down her back and two coming forward over her shoulders. She also has a unique face print that matches her head-tails piece.

SHAAK ATTACK

In the Legends of the *Star Wars* universe, Shaak Ti is defeated by Galen Marek. His minifigure appears only in Rogue Shadow (set 7672) from 2008, where he is named simply as 'Vader's apprentice'.

THE MORE ARMS I HAVE, THE MORE GOLD I CAN STEAL!

1 Unique head and shoulder piece

2 Huge, gaping mouth extends toward back of head

3 Extra limbs use same mold as LEGO® *Star Wars®* battle droid arms

FRENZY

MINI STATS

Theme
LEGO® Space

Year
2009

First appearance
Gold Heist (5971)

Rarity

Very definitely armed and dangerous, this space bandit is on the most-wanted list—both in the Space Police III subtheme and among minifigure collectors. If you spot his unique head peeking out of a box of LEGO bricks, expect a Frenzy!

MULTIPLE PLAYERS
Frenzy isn't the only LEGO minifigure with four arms. General Kozu (pictured), Lord Garmadon, and Pong Krell all have extra limbs.

MINI STATS

Theme
LEGO® Space

Years
1991–1992

First appearance
Two-Pilot Craft (1479)

Rarity

Rocketing into the LEGO Space theme in 1991, the Blacktron II Commander is an update of the original Blacktron minifigures from 1987. More colorful than his all-black predecessor, his enhancements include a jetpack accessory with twin handles.

THE NEW BLACK!

BLACKTRON II COMMANDER

I'M JOINING THE JET SET!

1 Same helmet and visor combo as M:Tron minifigures

2 New jetpack piece fits over torso

3 New Blacktron logo also worn by Blacktron Fan in THE LEGO® MOVIE™

COME FLY WITH ME

1991 also saw the release of an M:Tron minifigure with the new jetpack element.

Twi'lek and Jedi Knight Aayla Secura has a head piece with striped "lekku" head-tails at the back, and large eyes in the style of the animated TV series, *Star Wars®: The Clone Wars*. Her differently colored arms represent her one-sleeved top.

HEAD WITH TAILS!

MINI STATS

Theme
LEGO® *Star Wars®*

Year
2010

First appearance
Clone Turbo Tank (8098)

Rarity

AAYLA SECURA

IS IT COLD IN HERE?

1 New headgear mold with striped head-tails

2 Unique face print with large, *Clone Wars*-style eyes

3 Only a handful of minifigures have differently colored arms

4 Torso is also printed on the reverse

ONE OF VOS

Quinlan Vos is the Jedi Master who trained Aayla Secura. His minifigure has unique face and torso printing and is exclusive to 2011's Republic Frigate (set 7964).

LICENSE TO DRILL!

SPACE MINER

ALL BACK TO MINE!

MINER DETAIL
The LEGO® Space logo is hidden on the miner's armor, but with a drill in place of the rocket.

1 New helmet with clear visor

2 Orange ray gun element with detachable drill bit

3 Detailed printing includes steel toe caps

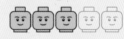

Not only does the Space Miner have a cool orange drill, he also has a new helmet and face print. His armor has been seen before, though: on Galaxy Patrol from Minifigures Series 7, Alien Avenger from Series 9, Lex Luthor from LEGO® DC Comics™ Super Heroes, and Infearno from LEGO® Ultra Agents.

"The color scheme went back and forth, but in the end we used almost the same colors as Luis Castañeda's concept sketch."
CHRIS B. JOHANSEN, LEGO DESIGN MASTER

MINI STATS

Theme
LEGO® Minifigures

Year
2014

First appearance
LEGO Minifigures Series 12

Rarity

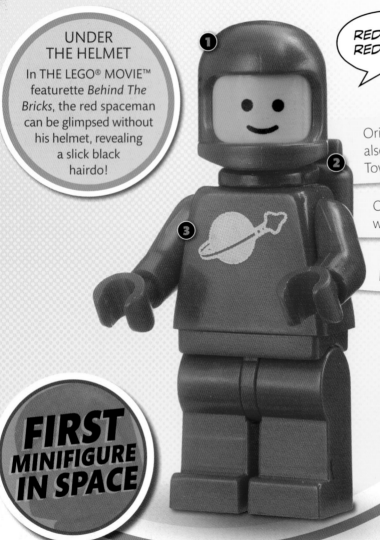

UNDER THE HELMET

In THE LEGO® MOVIE™ featurette *Behind The Bricks*, the red spaceman can be glimpsed without his helmet, revealing a slick black hairdo!

RED ALERT! RED ALERT!

1 Original helmet mold was also used in LEGOLAND Town and Castle sets

2 Oxygen tanks attached with a neck bracket

3 Iconic LEGO® Space logo is still used today

SPACEMAN

FIRST MINIFIGURE IN SPACE

The red spaceman and his fellow explorers signified a giant leap for LEGO minifigures. Boldly going where no bricks had gone before, they were the first to blast off into LEGOLAND Space. They also pioneered the visor-free helmet, which appeared in sets until 1988.

MINI STATS

Theme
LEGOLAND® Space

Years
1978–1986

First appearance
Rocket Launcher (462)

Rarity

SUITS YOU!

The red spaceman was the first to shoot for the stars, but the white, yellow, blue, and black spacemen quickly followed him. The black spaceman is the rarest, appearing in just eight sets.

The amphibian Gungan head that appears on this original LEGO *Star Wars* Jar Jar Binks was the first to be specially molded for a minifigure. The untidy vest and tunic printed on the torso are also unique to him.

FIRST SPECIAL HEAD!

HEADS UP

Since 1999, more than 30 unique head molds have been designed for LEGO *Star Wars* sets.

JAR JAR BINKS

MESA BE YOUSA MINIFIGURE, OKEEDAY?!

1 Head mold also used for Gungan Soldier in 2000

2 Finely sculpted eyelids add character to unprinted head piece

3 Long ears cover back of torso

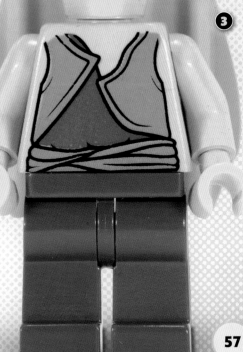

JAR JAR PINKS!

In 2011, Jar Jar got a slightly updated head mold, but it looks very different thanks to detailed printing that includes yellow and black eyes and a mottled pink pattern on the back of his ears.

BLUE SQUADRON

One of the Commander's Special Forces clone troopers was included with Jek-14's Stealth Starfighter (set 75018). He has similar printing, but on all-blue elements.

Available only with the DK book LEGO *Star Wars: The Yoda Chronicles*, this exclusive minifigure has a design inspired by early concept drawings for the stormtroopers from the *Star Wars* movies, made during the 1970s.

MINI STATS

Theme
LEGO® *Star Wars*®

Year
2013

First appearance
DK's LEGO *Star Wars: The Yoda Chronicles* book

Rarity

SPECIAL FORCES COMMANDER

I COMMAND YOUR ATTENTION!

1 Stormtrooper helmet mold with unique printing

2 Standard, scowling clone face under helmet

3 Torso print design continues onto hips

VADER'S FIST

Part of the 501st Legion, aka Vader's Fist, the elite Special Forces are distinguished from other clone troopers by the blue markings on their armor.

CLONE ALONE!

EIGHT-EYED ALIEN TOUGH!

SNAKE

I'M KEEPING MY EYES ON YOU!

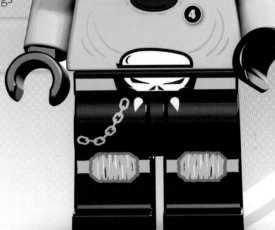

1 Spiked helmet is open at the back

2 Standard black visor can hide face—thankfully!

3 Head piece has seven eyes and four big fangs

4 Eighth eye in middle of torso

MINI STATS

Theme
LEGO® Space

Year
2009

First appearance
Space Truck Getaway
(5972)

Rarity

Snake is the most prolific bad guy in the Space Police III subtheme, featuring in four sets. His helmet has a movable visor that's perfect for hiding his identity. Which is just as well, as there's no mistaking his beady eyes—all eight of them!

GANGING UP

Snake is a member of the Black Hole Gang. This band of bad eggs is made up of criminals from the Space Police III subtheme, including Squidman, Frenzy, Kranxx, and the terrible Skull twins!

BARE FACED

Snake is identical in all his sets, except Space Speeder (set 8400), where he has no visor.

59

WE COME IN PIECES!

1 Helmet features an intricate wire pattern

2 Transparent red head piece beneath helmet is printed with menacing eyes

3 Bulky armor fits under head and adds height

ALPHA DRACONIS

WRITTEN IN THE STARS
The name of a real star, Alpha Draconis means "head of the dragon."

A major antagonist in the UFO subtheme, Alpha Draconis was one of the very first alien minifigures. This intergalactic baddie has an elaborate helmet, which you can remove—if you dare! Underneath is a head only a mother(ship) could love.

ALIEN INVASION

Alpha Draconis is the head of a race of aliens from the planet Humorless. These strange-looking, mind-reading beings came in red and blue variations.

MINI STATS

Theme
LEGO® Space

Year
1997

First appearance
Alien Avenger (6975)

Rarity

MINI STATS

Theme
LEGO® DC Comics™
Super Heroes

Year
2014

First appearance
San Diego Comic-Con
2014 giveaway

Rarity

This brightly colored Batman is an alien crime fighter from the planet Zur-en-Arrh! Part of an exclusive giveaway at the 2014 San Diego Comic-Con, he's the only Batman variant to carry a baseball bat.

"This Batman pops up a few times in comics, and we spent a lot of time trying to capture the characteristics of each appearance, to make him as awesome as possible!"

ADAM CORBALLY, LEGO
SENIOR GRAPHIC
DESIGNER

BATMAN OF ZUR-EN-ARRH

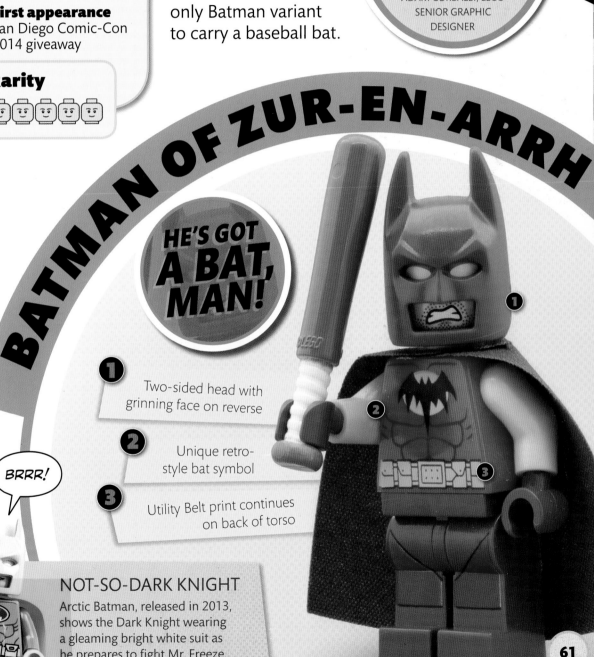

HE'S GOT A BAT, MAN!

1 Two-sided head with grinning face on reverse

2 Unique retro-style bat symbol

3 Utility Belt print continues on back of torso

BRRR!

NOT-SO-DARK KNIGHT
Arctic Batman, released in 2013, shows the Dark Knight wearing a gleaming bright white suit as he prepares to fight Mr. Freeze.

This robot has legs! Not just any old legs, either, but the very first printed legs and hips seen on a LEGO minifigure. An automated underling of the villainous forces of Spyrius (which gave the LEGO Space Spyrius subtheme its name), he also boasts a new robot face print, and a totally clear helmet with no visor—another minifigure first!

MINI STATS

Theme
LEGO® Space

Year
1994

First appearance
Lunar Launch Site
(6959)

Rarity

SPYRIUS DROID

I'M ALL WIRED OUT!

1 New transparent version of standard LEGO helmet

2 Head piece also used for a droid in the 1996 theme LEGO Time Cruisers

3 First-ever printed legs and hips

I SPY
The Spyrius Droid can be seen in the LEGO.com video *H.Q. Briefing*, where he wears a Space Police I uniform.

RISE OF THE ROBOTS
Spyrius was the first subtheme to cast minifigures as robots.

FIRST PRINTED LEGS

CHAPTER FOUR

YOU'RE MY HERO!

MEET THE MINIFIGURES WHO WILL FIGHT FOR WHAT'S RIGHT AND PROTECT US ALL FROM THE BAD GUYS!

NINJA, GO!

1 Same head wrap as Kai's ZX variant

2 Standard Kai face print with distinctive left-eye scar

3 Unique black kimono with red and gold pattern

NINJA WEAPON

This Kai variant wields a double-edged Fire blade.

The LEGO NINJAGO Ninja of Fire dons his elemental robes for the first and only time to date in Kai's Fire Mech. Kai's formal kimono is mostly black—unlike his original red robes—with the ninja's color used only for detail. His elemental robes are exclusive to this set.

MINI STATS

Theme
LEGO® NINJAGO™

Year
2013

First appearance
Kai's Fire Mech (70500)

Rarity

TAKING TO THE AIR

The Rattlecopter (set 9443) sees the ZX variant of Kai blasting into battle courtesy of an awesome rocket pack!

MINI STATS

Theme
LEGO® Star Wars®

Year
2012

First appearance
Republic Striker-class
Starfighter (9497)

Rarity

Strike a blow against the Sith with the Old Republic Jedi Satele Shan. This Jedi Knight minifigure is available only in the Republic Striker-class Starfighter, though her face print was also used for Wonder Woman in the LEGO® DC Comics™ Super Heroes theme, earlier in 2012.

WARRIOR WOMAN

SATELE SHAN

FIGHT ME AT YOUR PERIL!

1 Hair piece also worn by Agent Trace in LEGO® Agents

2 Reversible head piece with smiling face on reverse

3 Legs printed to suggest gray pants with green boots

4 Rare double-bladed lightsaber

SPARE PARTS

Satele Shan's droid companion, T7-O1, is unlike any other LEGO astromech droid—being made from 15 pieces instead of the standard four.

The Rock Raiders would be lost without their strong-willed pilot, Lieutenant Jet Marshall. The sole female member of this team of space travelers has appeared in seven Rock Raiders sets, and as a minifigure keychain.

SHE ROCKS!

MINI STATS

Theme
LEGO® Rock Raiders

Year
1999

First appearance
Light Hover (1274)

Rarity

JET MARSHALL

I'M ALWAYS IN CONTROL!

ROCK READERS
The first Rock Raiders sets all included special Rock Raiders comics.

1 Identical helmet to those worn by LEGO Exploriens

2 Blonde hair and headset printed on head piece

3 LEGO logo printed on back of torso

MINE CAST

Jet's fellow Raiders are: driver Axle; helmsman Bandit; commander Chief; geologist and explosives expert Docs; and mechanic Sparks.

RARE HEIR!

LET'S HUNT SOME ORC!

1

2

3

1 Unique head piece has a calm expression on reverse

2 Fabric cape is black on one side, red on the other

3 Torso printing depicts Evenstar necklace and White Tree of Gondor

ARAGORN

HERO HAIR
Aragorn's hair piece also appears in LEGO® *Prince of Persia*™ and LEGO® *Pirates of the Caribbean*™ sets.

The heroic defender of the Hobbits appears in four sets, but wears his royal garb in just one. This detailed variant has the same head and hair piece as the others, but now boasts a cape and intricate printed details that befit his status as heir of Gondor.

HO, STRIDER!
Aragorn wears his brown ranger's gear and carries a sword in every other set in which he appears. In Attack On Weathertop (set 9472), he also carries a flaming torch.

MINI STATS

Theme
LEGO® *The Lord of the Rings*™

Year
2013

First appearance
Battle at the Black Gate (79007)

Rarity

BOW DOWN TO ME OR SUFFER MY WRATH!

1 Molded hood over short fabric cape

2 Head can be turned around to reveal a worried look

3 Green "5" on torso is a clue to Lloyd's future as the fifth ninja

4 Shorter legs seen only on this version of the character

SON OF THE DARK LORD

Lloyd is the son of LEGO NINJAGO villain Lord Garmadon, but he grows up to be a good guy and fights against evil as the brave Green Ninja!

GOLDEN BOY
Young Lloyd is one of the only Lloyd variants not to wear mostly green. The other is the golden Ultimate Spinjitzu Master variant.

MINI STATS

Theme
LEGO® NINJAGO™

Year
2012

First appearance
Rattlecopter (9443)

Rarity

MINI STATS

Theme
LEGO® Star Wars®

Year
2015

First appearance
Ezra's Speeder Bike
(75090)

Rarity

Codenamed Spectre 5, this weapons expert is a key character in the *Star Wars Rebels*™ TV series. Her minifigure packs a real punch with unique printing, a special blue hair piece, and a pair of matching blaster pistols.

REBEL SPECTRE

SABINE WREN

DOWN WITH THE EMPIRE!

1 Unique blue and orange hair piece

2 Reversible head piece shows gritted teeth on reverse

3 Torso print shows Mandalorian armor with orange rebel symbol

REBEL FRIEND

Sabine Wren's fellow rebel Ezra Bridger also features in the Ezra's Speeder Bike set. He has a unique lightsaber with a hilt made from a binoculars piece.

69

Put on your Spectrespecs and take a closer look at this spellbinding minifigure. She's a unique character in many ways, and she's also the only Ravenclaw student to appear in a LEGO Harry Potter set. You really can't quibble with that!

GIN'S IN!

Both Luna and Ginny Weasley are exclusive to the Hogwarts Express set. Ginny also has two faces to choose from: a frown and a lopsided smile.

MINI

Theme
LEGO® Harry Potter™

Year
2010

First appearance
Hogwarts Express
(4841)

Rarity

HEX SPECS

In *Harry Potter*, Luna's Spectrespecs come free with wizarding newspaper, *The Quibbler*. The paper appears as a printed tile in the Hogwarts Express set.

LUNA LOVEGOOD

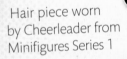

I'M RARER THAN A BLIBBERING HUMDINGER!

1 Hair piece worn by Cheerleader from Minifigures Series 1

2 Reverse of head piece shows smiling Luna without Spectrespecs

3 All-unique printing includes unusual skirt-over-pants legs

TOTALLY LOOONY!

HARD-TO-GET EMMET

HOWDY, HAT! HOWDY, PONCHO!

YOU'RE MY HERO!

EMMET (WILD WEST)

1 Hat designed in 2008 for Indiana Jones minifigure

2 Mustache is a cunning disguise

3 Unique fabric poncho design

4 Construction worker printing on legs and torso

Giddy-up and see if you can spot Emmet Brickowski in this clever cowboy disguise—complete with construction site ID card. This hard-to-find promotional minifigure was given away only with pre-orders of THE LEGO MOVIE video game.

NAP TIME!
Time to hit the hay? Emmet's ready for bed in his fancy-pants striped pajamas. This variant was also given away as a promotional set, and has a double-sided face print that shows him either winking or yawning.

MINI STATS

Theme
THE LEGO® MOVIE™

Year
2014

First appearance
Given away with THE LEGO MOVIE video game

Rarity

71

IS THIS A WIND-UP?

1 Hat mold created for LEGO® Pirates theme in 1989

2 Chin strap is printed on head

3 Key fits on to red neck bracket

4 Gold printing on arms and legs

TOY SOLDIER

MINI STATS

Theme
LEGO® Minifigures

Year
2013

First appearance
DK's LEGO *Minifigures Character Encyclopedia* book

Rarity

This rosy-cheeked fellow is found exclusively as part of the DK LEGO *Minifigures Character Encyclopedia* from 2013. He features a rare (and sadly non-functional!) wind-up key piece, and is the first character in the Minifigures series not to be part of a wider series.

MILITARY MATES

The Toy Soldier shares his military style with the Imperial Soldiers from the LEGO Pirates theme. These brave souls battle against Captain Redbeard and his scurvy crew!

MINI STATS

Theme
LEGO® *The Lord of the Rings*™

Year
2013

First appearance
The Council of Elrond (79006)

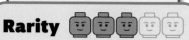

Rarity

Arwen appears in just one *The Lord of the Rings* set and is made up of all exclusive elements. Her character is noted for her beauty, and her minifigure is also a sight to behold, with an intricate new hair sculpt and detailed printing on her face, torso, and skirt.

COMPACT COUNCIL

At 243 pieces, the Council of Elrond set is one of the smallest in the LEGO *The Lord of the Rings* theme.

ELVISH EXCLUSIVE

ARWEN

FROM THE ASHES, A FIRE SHALL BE WOKEN.

1 New hair piece with pointed ears

2 Reversible head with angry face on other side

3 Slope piece with unique flowing dress print

ELF AWARE

The third variant of Arwen's father, Elrond, is also exclusive to The Council of Elrond set. Like his daughter, his printing is entirely unique.

Mon Mothma, the Supreme Commander of the Rebel Alliance, leads the rebel minifigures in their fight against the evil Empire. This LEGO® *Star Wars*® character is exclusive to the *Home One* Mon Calamari Star Cruiser set.

REBEL LEADER

Theme
LEGO® *Star Wars*®

Year
2009

First appearance
Home One Mon Calamari Star Cruiser (7754)

Rarity

MON MOTHMA

1

2

THE EMPIRE'S REIGN WILL SOON BE AT AN END!

NOBLE NECKLACE
Mon Mothma's printed torso features the Chandrilian Freedom Medal—a great honor from her home planet.

1

Hair piece also worn by Anakin Skywalker variant minifigure

2

Same face as original Princess Leia minifigure

3

White fabric cape

3

CAPED COMPANION
Also included in the same set as Mon Mothma is an exclusive Lando Calrissian minifigure in his general's uniform. Like Mon Mothma, he has a cape and a torso print based on his appearance in *Return of the Jedi*.

74

FLYIN' LION!

LAVAL

3... 2... 1... WE HAVE LIFT OFF!

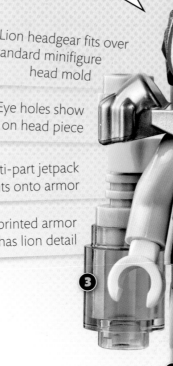

1 Lion headgear fits over standard minifigure head mold

2 Eye holes show printing on head piece

3 Multi-part jetpack fits onto armor

4 Unique printed armor on legs has lion detail

MINI STATS

Theme
LEGO® Legends of Chima™

Year
2013

First appearance
Scorm's Scorpion Stinger (70132)

Rarity

Laval, Prince of the Lion Tribe of Chima, comes in many variants, but only one has an awesome rocket-powered jetpack! The jetpack has eight parts, including two LEGO® *Star Wars*® lightsaber hilts, and appears in Scorm's Scorpion Stinger.

> "This minifigure was a challenge! Especially the element design—we had so many technical constraints."
>
> ALEXANDRE BOUDON, LEGO DESIGN MASTER

OUTLANDS DEFENDER

Laval appears in the same armor, minus the jetpack, while he's defending Lavertus's Outland Base (set 70134) from rival Tribes.

HAS ANYONE SEEN MY RAZOR?

1

2

3

TEAM PLAYERS

Dash Justice and his team also appeared in their own video game.

1 Brand new hair piece—since worn by Zane in LEGO® NINJAGO™ sets

2 Headset detail on unique face print

3 Detailed torso print with Alpha Team logo

DASH JUSTICE

DASH AND ALL

The Deep Sea variant of Dash has a diving helmet, while the stubble-free Deep Freeze variant dons fetching shades. However, they both sport Dash's trademark lopsided grin!

MINI STATS

Theme
LEGO® Alpha Team

Year
2001

First appearance
Alpha Team Helicopter (6773)

Rarity

Minifigures don't come much cooler than Dash Justice—secret agent and leader of the fearless Alpha Team. Dash has appeared in multiple variants, with different looks for many exciting missions. His detailed black suit is perfect for stealth operations.

MINI STATS

Theme
LEGO® NINJAGO™

Year
2011

First appearance
Nya (2172)

Rarity

Formidable warrior Nya is the sister of Kai, the Ninja of Fire. She was the first female minifigure in the NINJAGO theme, and one of the only NINJAGO minifigures to have a reversible head. Her alternative face shows a ninja mask covering her mouth.

FIRST LADY OF NINJAGO ISLAND!

NYA

I'M NOT LETTING THE BOYS HAVE ALL THE FUN!

 Hair piece first seen on Irina Spalko in LEGO® *Indiana Jones*™

 Reverse of head piece shows ninja mask

 Red robes with phoenix print echo those of her brother, Kai

WHOLE NEW WORLD

Nya has a cameo in THE LEGO® MOVIE™, as Wyldstyle is telling Emmet about all the realms in the LEGO universe.

THE X FACTOR

The Samurai X version of Nya has a helmet similar to Lord Garmadon's, but with a unique red part that covers her mouth. Underneath is another double-sided head—determined on one side, angry on the other.

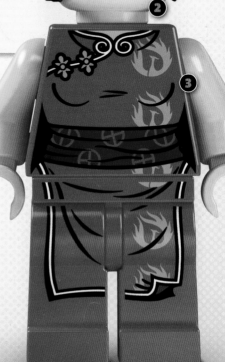

MINI STATS

Theme
LEGO® *The Hobbit*™

Year
2014

First appearance
Attack on Lake-town
(79016)

Rarity 😐 😐 😐 🙂 🙂

Tauriel is distinctive among the Elves in the LEGO® *The Hobbit*™ theme, thanks to her orange hair and freckled face printing. An earlier variant shared these features, but the most recent version has brighter torso and leg printing, and is unique to the Attack on Lake-town set.

ONLY ORANGE-HAIRED ELF

TAURIEL

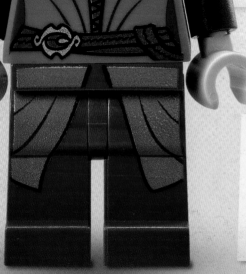

1 Hair piece is used on other Elves in different colors

2 Elven ears are part of head piece

3 Head can be turned to show a much angrier expression!

"That vivid green really makes Tauriel stand out within the murky Lake-town setting!"

DJORDJE DJORDJEVIC,
LEGO SENIOR
DESIGNER

ARMED TO THE TEETH

Tauriel carries the same bow accessory as fellow hero Bard the Bowman. Her earlier variant had twin silver and gold Elven knives, first seen in the LEGO® *Prince of Persia*™ theme.

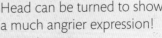

CHAPTER FIVE
SPOOKY
AND SCARY

BEWARE!
YOU ARE ABOUT
TO OPEN A VAULT
OF MINIFIGURE
FIENDS! DARE
YOU TURN
THE PAGE?

This smiling spirit proved very popular upon its 1990 release—and appeared in seven sets over five years, haunting the Black Knights, the Royal Knights, and even an old tree! Beneath the Ghost's new shroud piece is simply a white torso and a plain black head.

GLOWS IN THE DARK!

"I designed and sculpted the Ghost. In those days, that meant making a wooden prototype at five times actual size!"
NIELS MILAN PEDERSEN, LEGO DESIGNER

MINI STATS

Theme
LEGO® Castle

Years
1990, 1992–1993, 1995

First appearance
Black Monarch's Ghost (6034)

Rarity

GHOST

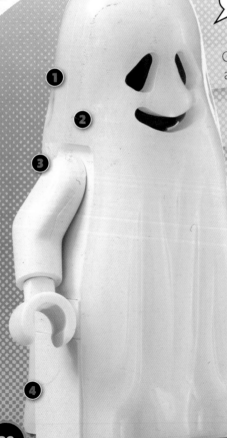

WOOOO!

1 Ghoulish face still has a classic LEGO smile!

2 Plain black head visible through mouth and eye holes

3 Glow-in-the-dark ghost piece slots over head and torso

4 1x2 brick and 1x2 plate instead of legs

A BIT PEEVED

Ghosts also play a big part in the world of Harry Potter, but the only one made into a minifigure has been Peeves The Poltergeist. He appeared in two sets in 2001.

HEAD BOLTS TOGETHER

THE MONSTER

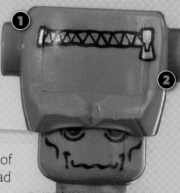

AARGH! A GHOST!

1 Unique head extension has LEGO studs on both sides

2 Zippers printed on front and back of head extension, and on back of head

3 Exclusive patchwork jacket print on torso

TALL STORY
The Monster was originally going to have 1x1 plates on his feet to make him taller.

Fittingly, this classic monster comes with an extra body part—a unique head extension. This monstrous forehead is printed with zippers at the front and back. Talk about getting down to the nuts and bolts!

MONSTERS, INC!
The Monster isn't the only minifigure with a screw or two loose. The Monster from Minifigures Series 4 and the Monster Butler from LEGO® Monster Fighters are both variations of this lumbering villain.

MINI STATS

Theme
LEGO® Studios

Year
2002

First appearance
Scary Laboratory (1382)

Rarity

1 It is rare for a minifigure to have no hat or hair

2 Dark stone-gray torso with medium stone-gray hands

3 Drumstick is longer than a regular LEGO turkey leg piece

4 Shovel design is unchanged since 1979!

ZOMBIE

FIRST ZOMBIE!

MINI STATS

Theme
LEGO® Minifigures

Year
2010

First appearance
LEGO Minifigures
Series 1

Rarity

The first ever zombie minifigure doesn't have much in the way of brains... He prefers a turkey leg! His inclusion in the first series of collectible Minifigures confirmed the eclectic nature of the theme, and pushed the boundaries of just what a minifigure could be.

HALLOWEEN HORROR
The Zombie also appears in Halloween Accessory Set (set 850487), but with a brown suit and a gray tie.

IT'S CATCHING!
Minifigures series 1 also introduced the Skateboarder, who has been reimagined as a zombie for this book.

MINI STATS

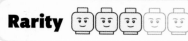

Theme
LEGO® The Lord
of the Rings™

Year
2013

First appearance
Pirate Ship Ambush
(79008)

Rarity

The cursed King of the Dead can never rest until he has fulfilled his oath to protect the land of Gondor. He is exclusive to just one LEGO The Lord of the Rings set, where he appears alongside two of his Soldiers of the Dead.

WHO GLOWS THERE?

KING OF THE DEAD

WHO ENTERS MY DOMAIN?

1 Unique sand-green crown

2 Glow-in-the-dark head piece has two expressions

3 Torso printed with ghoulish exposed ribs

4 Cloak also worn by Harry Potter's Quidditch variant

GHOSTLY GLOW

Glow-in-the-dark LEGO elements work by storing up light and releasing it slowly—giving a spooky white or green glow!

One of the henchmen of evil genius Dr. Inferno, Slime Face just wants to recover sunken treasure—if only the LEGO Agents would leave him alone! The minifigure's head is colored trans-neon green to make it look like slimy green jelly.

YUCKY-LOOKING VILLAIN!

MINI STATS

Theme
LEGO® Agents

Year
2008

First appearance
Deep Sea Quest
(8636)

Rarity

SLIME FACE

① ②

I'M SORRY, I HAVE A BAD COLD

① Rare helmet also worn by Mr. Freeze in LEGO® DC Comics™ Super Heroes

② Transparent green head with slime printing

③ Dr. Inferno's logo— a scary burning skull!

"The eyes and mouth really stand out. The one red eye is a vibrant contrast to the slime."
LAUGE DREWES, LEGO DESIGN MANAGER

CRUDE CREW

Slime Face isn't Dr. Inferno's only mean-looking crony: Break Jaw and Gold Tooth also have uniquely evil appearances!

SPOOKY GIRL

1 Unique hair piece extends down front and back of torso

2 Spider emerging from pocket

3 Teddy bear element is also carried by the Panda Guy Minifigure— naturally his is black and white, too!

4 Gray fabric skirt

ALL
BLACK
AND
WHITE

Spooky Girl is made of only black, white, and gray elements—the most noticeable being her new hair piece. She wears a black jacket and her legs are printed with stripy socks. She is the fifth collectible Minifigure to have a teddy bear, though only hers has one eye missing.

THE MONOCHROME SETS

Spooky Girl is the third monochrome collectible Minifigure. The first was the Mime from Series 2, and the second was the Sad Clown from Series 10.

MINI STATS

Theme
LEGO® Minifigures

Year
2014

First appearance
LEGO Minifigures Series 12

Rarity

FANCY A BITE?

ICONIC HORROR VILLAIN

1 New slicked-back hair piece

2 Head can be turned around to reveal an open mouth

3 Flowing cape is red on one side, brown on the other

VAMPIRE

HAIR HEIR
The Vampire's hair has since been worn by Wolverine from LEGO® Marvel Super Heroes.

BITE-SIZED FACT
Slay one vampire and another takes its place. Thankfully, the Vampire from the second series of collectible Minifigures is far from your average bloodsucker, favoring a fruit smoothie to a pint of the red stuff.

 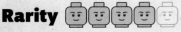
This caped count has developed quite a "fang" club over the years. Not only is he the original vampire minifigure, he's also the first to have a combed widow's peak hair piece. His double-sided head shows either his toothy smile, or him opening his mouth in anticipation of a juicy neck.

MINI STATS

Theme
LEGO® Minifigures

Year
2015

First appearance
LEGO Minifigures
Series 14

Rarity

The Minifigures theme has regularly featured characters dressed up in strange costumes. In the past we've seen minifigures dressed as bunnies, chickens, gorillas—and even hot dogs. But a guy dressed as a man-eating plant? Now that's a first!

BEYOND BE-LEAF!

PLANT MONSTER

EAT YOUR GREENS—BEFORE THEY EAT YOU!

1 Terrified expression—is this monster scared of itself?

2 Unique carnivorous plant piece surrounds head

3 Dark green legs and torso are the same color as most LEGO trees and plants

WHY WORRY?

The Plant Monster is not the first character in the Minifigures line to look worried. Hazmat Guy has a similar expression, despite his protective suit!

TACKLE THE JACKALS

Helping the Flying Mummy to guard Scorpion Pyramid (set 7327) are two Anubis Guards. These jackal-headed warriors each carry a sword and a scarab shield.

Unearthed in 2011 as part of the Pharaoh's Quest theme, the Flying Mummy has a truly extravagant wing piece. It attaches to the minifigure's neck and features 22 tan feathers and 18 blue ones.

MINI STATS

Theme
LEGO® Pharaoh's Quest

Year
2011

First appearance
Flying Mummy Attack (7307)

Rarity

FLYING MUMMY

1
Falcon headdress resembles Ancient Egyptian god Horus

2
Reverse of head shows just one unbandaged eye

3
Elaborate printed wings attach with a neck bracket over the minifigure's neck

1

2

COME FLY WITH ME! MUMMY BACK GUARANTEED!

3

SPECTACULAR
WING
PIECE

DAWN OF THE WED!

I DON'T MEAN TO MOAN, BUT...

1 No other minifigure wears a ponytail in this tan color

CORDON BLEURGH!
The Monster Fighters theme also includes a Zombie Chef!

2 Reversible head shows open mouth on other side

3 Unique torn bridal gown print on slope piece and torso

ZOMBIE BRIDE

On her big day, the Zombie Bride is dressed to digest in her unusual sloped piece, printed like a dilapidated wedding gown. Minifigures should be careful if they receive an invite to her wedding— it might just be them on the menu...

LOVE AT FIRST FRIGHT
The Zombies set is well named, featuring not only a Zombie Bride, but also a top-hatted Zombie Groom, and a Zombie Driver in a tattered chauffeur's uniform.

MINI STATS

Theme
LEGO® Monster Fighters

Year
2012

First appearance
The Zombies (9465)

Rarity

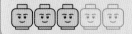

DON'T TELL ANYONE, BUT I CAN'T SWIM!

① Helmet hides fishy facial features!

② Armor and helmet are black with gold printing

③ Portal key is one element

RUST IN PEACE!

PORTAL EMPEROR

One of the six guardian races of the underwater world of Atlantis, the Portal Emperor includes a new helmet with a never-before-seen gold and black speckled paint pattern. This minifigure is made of five parts, four of which are unique.

PORTAL KEYS

All but two of the LEGO Atlantis sets come with specially molded portal keys, which were the object of the divers' quest in the 2010 storyline.

MINI STATS

Theme
LEGO® Atlantis

Year
2010

First appearance
Portal of Atlantis (8078)

 **Rarity**

MINI STATS

Theme
LEGO® Harry Potter™

Year
2005

First appearance
Graveyard Duel
(4766)

Rarity

You won't know whether to say "accio" or "evanesco" when you see this frightening minifigure! This variant of You-Know-Who wears a Death Eater's robe and has clear eyes in his glow-in-the-dark head. He actually looks OK for someone trapped in limbo...

THE DARK LORD!

LORD VOLDEMORT

1 Glow-in-the-dark head piece

2 Cloak also worn by Dementor minifigures

3 Black torso and legs under robe

1

2

3

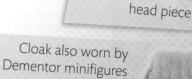

NOSE TO NOSE

Lord Voldemort is one of the few LEGO minifigures to have a nose of sorts, yet his character has lost his!

SLYTHERIN IN!

Hinting at a future as Lord Voldemort, the Tom Riddle minifigure from The Chamber of Secrets (set 4730), is the only Slytherin minifigure to wear a black cape.

91

NO BODY COMES CLOSE!

This spooky fellow is ready for the scariest night of the year! Skeleton Guy pays tribute to the enduring LEGO Skeleton figure, but this time in actual minifigure form. He's especially notable for those rare printed arms and his creepy pumpkin basket. Trick or treat!

MINI STATS

Theme
LEGO® Minifigures

Year
2015

First appearence
LEGO Minifigures Series 14

Rarity

SKELETON GUY

I'D LIKE TO SCARE PEOPLE BUT I DON'T HAVE THE GUTS!

1 Skeleton mask with side strings

2 Printing designed to look like LEGO Skeleton figures

3 Printing on arms and sides of legs is a rare detail

"Some years ago, I made a drawing of how I thought Skeleton Guy should look, and apart from the eyes, the design didn't change much."

CHRIS B. JOHANSEN,
LEGO DESIGN MASTER

SPECIAL UNDEAD VARIANT

UURR... MUST... DO... OLLIE!

ZOMBIE SKATEBOARDER

1 Same expression as Series 1 Skateboarder

2 Skull print now has "dead" X-shaped eyes

3 Studs hold minifigure on skateboard

The first Skateboarder minifigure was part of Minifigures Series 1, but this zombie version is available only with this book. His red eyes and gray skin color mark him out as the latest in a long line of LEGO zombies, which also began in Series 1.

"I always like it when we reimagine existing characters, so we can see what happened to them. I guess this guy wasn't such a good skater in the end..."

CHRIS B. JOHANSEN, LEGO DESIGN MASTER

MINI STATS

Theme
LEGO® Minifigures

Year
2015

First appearance
DK's *I Love That Minifigure* book

Rarity

> I KNOW YOUR EVERY MOVE...

1 Long, blood-red hairpiece

2 Same face as the chess set's Evil Bishop

3 Skeleton armor resembles ribs

4 Plain black slope instead of legs

EVIL QUEEN

Released as part of the Fantasy Era Castle Chess Set, the Evil Queen, alongside the Evil Wizard, leads a skeleton army against the Crown King. She has long hair which covers a red-eyed skeletal head, and a torso piece featuring armor with a skull motif.

MINI STATS

Theme
LEGO® Castle

Year
2007

First appearance
Castle Chess Set
(852001)

Rarity

WITCH SWITCH

The Castle Giant Chess Set (set 852293) from 2008 replaced the Evil Queen with an Evil Witch, who was also in the 2008 LEGO Castle Advent Calendar (set 7979)—so the Evil Queen is rarer!

MINI STATS

Theme
LEGO® *The Lord of the Rings*™

Year
2013

First appearance
Battle at the Black Gate (79007)

Rarity

Sauron's own messenger has a head piece printed with wrinkly skin, a large mouth full of snarling teeth, but no eyes. His elaborate helmet is as specific to him as the printing on his head, legs, and torso.

UNIQUE HORNED HELMET

MOUTH OF SAURON

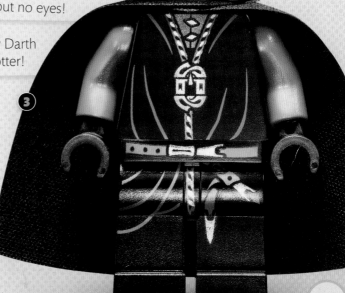

SAURON THE GREAT, BIDS THEE WELCOME!

1 Unique helmet resembles Mordor architecture

2 Head printed with bared teeth—but no eyes!

3 Black cape also worn by Darth Vader and Harry Potter!

MORDOR MOB
Two different Mordor Orc minifigures appear with the Mouth of Sauron in Battle at the Black Gate. One has brown skin, the other green.

SCARY SKULL!

This frightening-looking minifigure sends shivers down the spine! A variant of the Skeleton Drone that first appeared in LEGO Alpha Team in 2002, the Super Ice Drone has a unique black skull head piece with white printing and red eyes, and its uniform features a silver-lined scarab with a cross.

MINI STATS

Theme
LEGO® Alpha Team

Year
2005

First appearance
Scorpion Orb Launcher (4774)

Rarity

SUPER ICE DRONE

①

②

WHY THE COLD SHOULDER?

① Unique scary face print

② Transparent blue helmet exclusive to Alpha Team

③ Rare mismatched arm and leg colors

③

WHAT'S IN A NAME?

The Super Ice Drone is controlled by the villainous Ogel, whose name spelled backward is LEGO. This bad guy was given this name because he represents the opposite of LEGO fun and play.

CHAPTER SIX
THE WORLD'S A STAGE

ROLL UP!
ROLL UP! PREPARE
TO BE AMAZED BY
THE SHOW-OFFS
AND ENTERTAINERS
OF THE LEGO
WORLD!

GIVE US A HISS!

① New turban element

② Unique face print with waxed mustache

③ Long shirttails printed on legs

④ New cobra accessory

SNAKE CHARMER

This collectible Minifigure is every bit the traditional Snake Charmer, with his white turban and waxed mustache. He comes with a "pungi" flute—and a rubber cobra, of course!

SSSLITHERING SSSNAKESSS!

The Snake Charmer Mummy from LEGO® Pharaoh's Quest is another minifigure able to control snakes. Unfortunately, this bandaged baddie only uses his skills for evil!

Nightclub singer Willie Scott wears a glamorous, Chinese-inspired outfit when she is swept up in an adventure with Indiana Jones. The pretty dress is not very practical for battling baddies—no wonder Willie's dual-sided head turns from smiling to scared!

GREAT SCOTT!

WILLIE SCOTT

1 Tiara slots into unique hair piece

2 Double-sided face— smiling or scared!

3 Diamond accessory

4 Unique sequinned dress printing on torso and legs

DIAMONDS ARE MY BEST FRIENDS!

ALL MINE!

The Temple of Doom (set 7199) features Willie with different hair and unique printing—ill-suited for her trip in a runaway mine cart!

COSMIC CLUB

Willie meets Indy in Club Obi Wan— named after Obi-Wan Kenobi from *Star Wars*!

The cheerful Hula Dancer from LEGO Minifigures Series 3 comes with a black hair piece with a flower printed on one side. A new grass skirt design covers her green hips, and her legs have printed green briefs, similar to the Lifeguard's red uniform in Series 2.

MORE MARACAS

Lime-green maracas also appear in Ariel's Undersea Palace (set 41063), released in 2015.

MINI STATS

Theme
LEGO® Minifigures

Years
2011–2012

First appearance
LEGO Minifigures Series 3

Rarity

HULA DANCER

ALOHA, EVERYBODY!

1 Flower print on hair piece

2 New maraca accessory

3 Unique "grass" skirt

4 Printed green briefs hidden under skirt

BEACH PARTY

The Hula Dancer was also included in the Minifigure Beach Accessory Pack (set 850449) along with two surfers, and a beach barbecue assembly.

FLOWER IN HER HAIR

NEW DRAGON DESIGN

HEY, EVERYONE! CHECK OUT MY NINJA SKILLS!

1
Head wrap has rear clip to hold katana blade

2
Unique torso and leg printing depicts Jay's lightning power

3
Back of torso has Jay's name in gold

2-DX
Jay DX appears in just two sets: Skeleton Bowling and Lightning Dragon Battle (set 2521).

JAY DX

The DX variant of the LEGO NINJAGO Ninja of Lightning has the same head wrap and face as the original Jay minifigure, but comes with sleek new torso and leg printing. DX stands for Dragon eXtreme, so the design features a dragon breathing lightning.

RAW ENERGY
The NRG Jay minifigure sees the NINJAGO warrior transformed into pure lightning energy. Talk about a bolt from the blue!

MINI STATS

Theme
LEGO® NINJAGO™

Year
2011

First appearance
Skeleton Bowling (2519)

Rarity

CROSS MY PALM WITH SILVER STUDS

1 Hair, purple bandana, and golden beads are all one element

2 Tower tarot card is printed on a 1x2 tile

3 Dark-red slope piece with detailed printing

ALL UNIQUE PARTS

Every element that makes up the Fortune Teller minifigure is special to her, from the printed torso and sloped skirt to her hair piece with purple bandana and golden beads attached—not to mention her two tarot cards. Her serene expression suggests she is about to make a bold prediction...

MINI STATS

Theme
LEGO® Minifigures

Year
2013

First appearance
LEGO Minifigures Series 9

Rarity

NOT ALL DOOM AND GLOOM

As well as the Tower card, which warns of impending disaster, the Fortune Teller also carries the Sun card, which foretells good fortune.

For many years there were no minifigures with yellow hair, because it would have been the same color as their faces. A lighter color known as "cool yellow" was introduced in 1999 and has been used on a succession of blonde minifigures—but few wear it as timelessly as the Hollywood Starlet!

MINI STATS

Theme
LEGO® Minifigures

Year
2013

First appearance
LEGO Minifigures
Series 9

Rarity

AND THE AWARD FOR...

The Hollywood Starlet was the fourth collectible Minifigure to come with a minifigure-shaped trophy, after the Karate Master, the Sumo Wrestler, and the Soccer Player.

HOLLYWOOD STARLET

I'M READY FOR MY CLOSE-UP NOW...

LOOKALIKE

The Hollywood Starlet could almost be mistaken for the legendary movie star Marilyn Monroe.

1 New blonde hair piece

2 Gold minifigure trophy

3 All exclusive printing

4 Slope piece represents floor-length gown

Peabody Public Library
Columbia City, IN

BLONDE ON YELLOW!

Jesting, jesting, one two three... The 2012 Harley Quinn minifigure is let loose alongside her occasional boyfriend (and Batman's archest enemy) The Joker in The Dynamic Duo Funhouse Escape. Harley's minifigure consists of almost entirely new parts, although her red and black jester's hat, with white pom-poms, first appeared on her 2008 minifigure.

MINI **STATS**

Theme
LEGO® DC Comics™
Super Heroes

Year
2012

First appearance
The Dynamic Duo
Funhouse Escape (6857)

Rarity

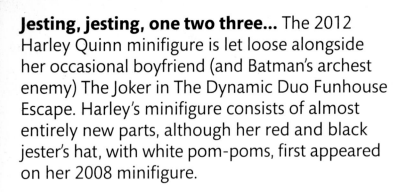

HARLEY QUINN

JEST FOR THE WICKED!

1 Harley's jester's hat is unique to her character

2 Unusual mismatched arms, hands, and legs

3 Diamond print is bigger than on 2008 Harley variant

NOT-MUCH-BETTER HALF

Harley Quinn's alter ego, Dr. Harleen Quinzel, appears in 2013's Arkham Asylum Breakout (set 10937).

WINGS FOR ARMS!

> YOU CRACK ME UP... AND THAT'S NO YOLK!

1 Unique chicken head piece

2 Minifigure face shows through mask

3 Unique molded wings for arms

EGGSACTLY THE SAME

The torso and wings look exactly the same from the front and the back.

CHICKEN SUIT GUY

WILD ABOUT ANIMALS!

Chicken Suit Guy is the fourth animal costume collectible Minifigure, following Gorilla Suit Guy, Lizard Man, and Bunny Suit Guy.

The new hat piece worn by the wacky Chicken Suit Guy—complete with beak, comb, and wattles—is not the only element that had never been seen before he was hatched. His wing-shaped arms are also a brand-new mold exclusive to him.

MINI STATS

Theme
LEGO® Minifigures

Year
2013

First appearance
LEGO Minifigures Series 9

Rarity

105

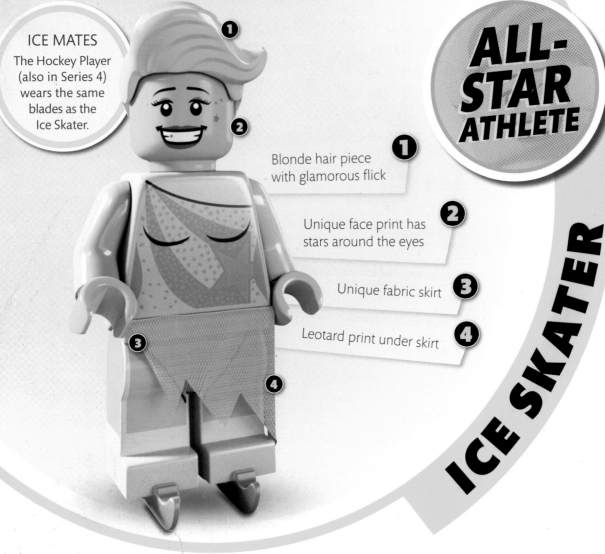

ALL-STAR ATHLETE

ICE SKATER

1 Blonde hair piece with glamorous flick

2 Unique face print has stars around the eyes

3 Unique fabric skirt

4 Leotard print under skirt

With her winning smile and winning attitude—not to mention her new blonde bun hair piece—the Ice Skater makes quite an impression. She has a distinctive fabric skirt, and her torso has one blue arm and one yellow arm, for a stylish off-the-shoulder look.

FANCY FROCK
Just like Kimono Girl, Cave Woman, and many others, the Ice Skater's torso is printed front and back. Her new hair mold has since been worn by the Fairy and the Flamenco Dancer.

MINI STATS

Theme
LEGO® DC Comics™
Super Heroes

Year
2014

First appearance
The Tumbler
(76023)

Rarity

Modeled on the *Dark Knight* movie character, this variant of Batman's arch-enemy appears in just one set. He has messier hair than other Joker minifigures, as well as fading face paint and a stern mouth beneath a false grin.

DARK KNIGHT VILLAIN

WHY SO SERIOUS?

THE JOKER

1 Hair piece also seen on Anakin Skywalker minifigure—in brown

2 Serious face print—other Joker variants have grins

3 Green tie instead of usual Joker neckerchief

4 Overcoat printing continues onto legs

THE JOKERS IN THE PACK

There are also LEGO® DUPLO® and microfigure versions of The Joker, plus several minifigure variants including this Asylum Inmate in bright-orange prison fatigues.

In robes emblazoned with moons and stars, the Wizard looks every inch the arcane sorcerer. He is one of only three collectible Minifigures to be made up of ten pieces—the other two being the Hockey Player and the Bride.

IT'S NOT A DRESS!

The Wizard is the first male in the Minifigures series to have a slope piece instead of regular legs.

MINI STATS

Theme
LEGO® Minifigures

Year
2014

First appearance
LEGO Minifigures Series 12

Rarity

WIZARD

AND FOR MY NEXT TRICK...

1 New conical hat with metallic printing

2 Three-piece staff includes telescope and jewel elements

3 Fabric cape and collar are two separate pieces

4 Beard and mustache piece fits around neck

HAIRY MAGIC

If that beard looks familiar, it's because it was also used for Gandalf the Grey in *The Lord of the Rings*™ theme in 2012. It must be the height of fashion among wizards!

WHERE ARE MY PANTS? GUY

1 Grin—he sure looks happy for someone who has lost his pants!

WHERE ARE MY... OH!

2 Spare pair of white legs as an accessory. Make sure you don't lose them!

3 Bare legs with white underwear

SPARE PAIR OF LEGS!

MINI STATS

Theme
THE LEGO® MOVIE™

Year
2014

First appearance
LEGO Minifigures
The LEGO MOVIE
Series

Rarity

"Where are my pants?"
They're in your hand, guy! The first minifigure to come with two pairs of legs also has an exclusive Hawaiian shirt print— perfect for such a larger-than- life character.

HAIR ROCKS!
Where Are My Pants? Guy has the same hair piece as Frank Rock from LEGO® Monster Fighters and the Mechanic from LEGO® Minifigures Series 6, both from 2012.

DANGER IS MY MIDDLE NAME!

1 Cool new hair piece

2 Devil-may-care face printing includes raised eyebrow and megawatt grin

3 "MF" on belt buckle stands for minifigure—or LEGO designer Michael Fuller

4 Helmet can be worn instead of hair piece

DAREDEVIL

HAIR OR HELMET?

Just two other collectible Minifigures have helmets and hair pieces: Intergalactic Girl and the Race Car Driver.

The Daredevil is all about style—check out his coiffured hair, handlebar mustache, and red, white, and blue jumpsuit. His head has two faces: a cockily confident one, and a far more appropriately worried expression...

MINI STATS

Theme
LEGO® Minifigures

Year
2012

First appearance
LEGO Minifigures Series 7

Rarity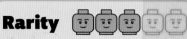

CHAPTER SEVEN

ONE OF A KIND

SOME MINIFIGURES ARE JUST A LITTLE BIT DIFFERENT. THESE CHARACTERS REALLY STAND OUT FROM THE CROWD!

Dwarves love their food, and this short-legged minifigure from the LEGO® *The Hobbit*™ theme has a special piece that combines his hair, his beard, and his round belly. Known as a "sandwich board," this unique element gives Bombur the appearance of being very well fed!

COMPANY OF DWARVES

All of the dwarves who set out to reclaim the kingdom of Erebor have been made into minifigures. They appear across eight different LEGO *The Hobbit* sets.

EXTRA BELLY PIECE

BOMBUR THE DWARF

WHAT'S FOR DINNER?

1 Double-sided face printing

2 The torso piece under Bombur's beard replicates his tunic's stitches.

3 Short legs

MINI STATS

Theme
LEGO® *The Hobbit*™

Year
2012

First appearance
An Unexpected Gathering (79003)

STAND-UP GUY
Bombur's short legs are unposable, so he eats standing up in An Unexpected Gathering.

Rarity

SAUSAGE SANDWICH BOARD!

> I APPROACH MY JOB WITH RELISH!

1 Unique "sandwich board" piece shaped like a hot dog

2 Cheerful expression... Mmm, hot dogs!

3 Plain tan torso matches bun color

> "The initial design didn't have any mustard, but the final version has just the right amount of zig-zag sauce!"
>
> GITTE THORSEN, LEGO DESIGN MASTER

HOT DOG GUY

There's never been a Minifigure quite like this character! His detailed hot dog outfit is all one piece and fits over the minifigure's head like any other headgear. Maybe he sells hot dogs, or perhaps he just really likes them!

HOT DOGS! GET YOUR HOT DOGS!

Released in 2013, the LEGO® Creator Hot Dog Stand (set 40078) was free to VIP members of LEGO.com with qualifying purchases. The set included a hot dog chef.

MINI STATS

Theme
LEGO® Minifigures

Year
2015

First appearance
LEGO Minifigures Series 13

Rarity
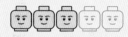

113

HAPPY NEW YEAR! The "Y2K" on this minifigure's torso represents the year 2000.

FIRST LEGO® LEAGUE GUY

FIRST

LEGO

Y2K

1 No hat or hair piece—just shades!

2 Printing on back lists schools taking part in the scheme

3 A 1999 variant has white legs, tan arms, and a thin mustache

MINI STATS

Theme
N/A

Year
2000

First appearance
Given to participants in FIRST LEGO® League

Rarity

This rare minifigure was available as part of the FIRST LEGO League educational initiative, which aims to engage and educate children through play. Issued in 2000 to mark the new millennium, he is unusual in having no hair piece, but what he lacks in locks he makes up for in cool shades.

TO THE STARS!

In 2006, FIRST LEGO League groups were invited to explore nanotechnology with Nano Quest (set 9763). It included two astronaut minifigures, both sporting the torso piece first seen on Hikaru from LEGO® EXO-FORCE™.

Treasure hunters pay attention!

You've hit the jackpot if you find a Mr. Gold among your Minifigures. Mr. Gold has a gold face, gold torso, gold leg piece, and gold hat. The only parts that aren't glistening with a chrome gold finish are his white-gloved hands!

5,000 FOR 10

Created to mark the 10th series of collectible Minifigures, only 5,000 of Mr. Gold were ever made. No one knows if all of them have all been found. Do you have one in your collection?

GLOBE TROTTER

Anyone who found Mr. Gold in 2013 was invited to enter their location on LEGO.com to record where he turned up!

MR. GOLD

> I DARE SAY IT'S YOUR LUCKY DAY!

1 No other minifigure has a gold top hat!

2 Unique glad-to-be-gold expression

3 White hands can grasp his golden cane

MINI STATS

Theme
LEGO® Minifigures

Year
2013

First appearance
LEGO Minifigures Series 10

CHROME SWEET CHROME

 **Rarity**

NOSE AND ARROWS

The striking Native American is unusual because she is the only member of her tribe to not wear face paint. She and her fellow LEGO Western tribe members introduced never-before-seen feather headdresses and the black braided hair piece.

MINI STATS

Theme
LEGO® Western

Year
1997, 2002

First appearance
Chief's Tepee (6746)

Rarity

NATIVE AMERICAN

I'M ALL A-QUIVER AT BEING IN THIS BOOK!

1 Feathers slot into hair piece

2 LEGO Western minifigures had rare nose printing

3 Unique torso print

TARGET MARKET
More than 70 minifigures have carried a quiver of arrows.

NEW NATIVE
The Medicine Man has the same legs as the female tribe member. He sports a new buffalo headdress, too.

GOING FOR GOLD!

DING-DING! SECONDS OUT, ROUND 2!

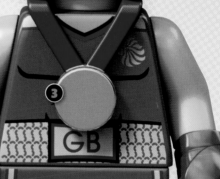

BRAWNY BOXER

1 Same headguard mold as Series 5 Boxer

2 Confident grin shows blue gumshield

3 Detachable gold medal

4 Boxing gloves instead of standard hands

FASTER, HIGHER, STRONGER

Eight other sporting disciplines were represented in the Team GB Minifigures series: judo, gymnastics, tennis, horse-riding, swimming, archery, weightlifting, and relay.

Produced for the 2012 London Olympics, the Brawny Boxer was part of the Team GB Minifigures subtheme, available only in the UK and Ireland. His exclusive printing includes his torso and headguard, both of which feature the Team GB lion's head logo.

MINI STATS

Theme
LEGO® Minifigures

Year
2012

First appearance
LEGO Minifigures Team GB Series

Rarity

117

HALLO!

DE BOUWSTEEN GUY

1 Back of torso printed with LEGO logo

2 De Bouwsteen logo is a happy builder

3 Rare dark-blue hands

DE BOUWSTEEN

GOING DUTCH
De Bouwsteen is Dutch for "the building block."

De Bouwsteen is the LEGO fan club of the Netherlands—and the biggest LEGO fan club in the world! Since 2001, the Netherlands has hosted the annual "LEGO World" fan event, and for the 2005 show, 1,000 special De Bouwsteen minifigures were produced, each one coming with its own certificate.

MINI STATS

Theme
N/A

Year
2005

First appearance
Specially produced for LEGO® World fan event

Rarity

2008 MODEL
Another De Bouwsteen minifigure was made in 2008. He wears a red shirt and has wispy red hair poking out from under his peaked cap. Only 750 were made, so he is also highly sought-after.

MINI STATS

Theme
LEGO® NINJAGO™

Year
2014

First appearance
NinjaCopter (70724)

Rarity

Primary Interactive X-ternal Assistant Life-form, or P.I.X.A.L., was created as a robot aide for an evil inventor in the world of LEGO NINJAGO, but soon lent her helping hands to the Ninja instead. Assembled in 2014, she appears in just one set.

RARE ROBOT

P.I.X.A.L.

TWO HEADS ARE BETTER THAN ONE!

1 Gray hair piece is silver in the LEGO NINJAGO TV show.

2 Double-sided face print with evil red eyes on reverse

3 All-exclusive printing

A TOXIC ENEMY!

Toxikita, the sneaky villainess from LEGO® Ultra Agents, uses the same hair piece as P.I.X.A.L. but in green.

TAKE YOUR P.I.X.

In the LEGO NINJAGO TV show, inventor Cyrus Borg created 15 P.I.X.A.L. prototypes before this one, but they all went wrong!

This dapper chap is the leader of a brave band of Monster Fighters, all of whom have exclusive head and torso prints. His fellow fighters also had brand new printing on their legs, but Rodney goes one better, with a whole new leg entirely! His robotic right limb is completely unique.

UNIQUE ROBOT LEG!

MINI STATS

Theme
LEGO® Monster Fighters

Year
2012

First appearance
The Vampyre Hearse (9464)

Rarity

DR. RODNEY RATHBONE

I CAP HOP FASTER THAN I CAN RUN!

1 New bowler hat element

2 Red moonstone gives power to Rodney's enemy, Lord Vampyre

3 Steam-powered artificial leg!

BLAZING BIKE
Rodney rides a red motorcycle while in hot pursuit of The Vampyre Hearse.

SQUARE AND RARE!

BEEP-BOOP! WHO-WANTS-A-HUG?

CLOCKWORK ROBOT

1 Rectangular head mold shared with Lady Robot from Minifigures Series 11

2 Wind-up key attaches to neck bracket

3 Printed details includes torso rivets and toecaps

GET A-HEAD
Minifigures Series 6 introduced three new head molds: for Clockwork Robot, Classic Alien, and Minotaur.

What makes a Minifigure tick? In this case, it's the key in his back! This rarely seen piece attaches to a neck bracket by means of a sideways stud. His rectangular head piece has a mouth full of sparking lights and glowing blue eyes that match his colorful torso print.

SILVER STREAK

The Clockwork Robot was preceded by the Robot from Minifigures Series 1, released in 2010. He has twin antennas and a special tool arm.

MINI STATS

Theme
LEGO® Minifigures

Year
2012

First appearance
LEGO Minifigures Series 6

Rarity

I'M YOUR CZECH MATE!

① Hair piece worn by various Weasleys in Harry Potter sets

② Torso design celebrates Kladno facility's brick-decoration specialism

③ Back of torso shows LEGO® logo and the word "Kladno"

ONLY 2000 EXIST!

KLADNO GUY

TOP SPEED
The Kladno facility can produce up to 16,000 minifigures every hour!

MINI STATS

Theme
N/A

Year
2014

First appearance
N/A

Kladno is a town in the Czech Republic, home to one of the LEGO Group's manufacturing facilities. In 2013, its employees designed a minifigure and this cheerful fellow was given to the factory workers at Christmas.

POTTED PLANT
When the Kladno plant was completed in 2012, The LEGO Group produced a LEGO version of the complex, which was also given out to employees.

MINI STATS

Theme
LEGO® *Star Wars*®

Year
2013

First appearance
Homing Spider Droid
(75016)

Rarity

Tholothian Jedi Master
Stass Allie is the first of her species to appear in minifigure form. Featured in just one LEGO *Star Wars* set, she wears a unique Tholoth headdress with distinctive fleshy tendrils.

A HEAD-DRESS TO IMPRESS!

STASS ALLIE

BRING ON THE BATTLE DROIDS!

1 Rubber headdress fits over head piece

2 Unique Jedi robe print continues on back of torso

3 Lightsaber blade also used as a uranium rod in LEGO® The Simpsons™ sets

HEAD OF THE CLASS
Stass Allie isn't the only LEGO *Star Wars* minifigure to have elaborate headgear. Ahsoka Tano is one of two minifigures to have colorful Togruta head-tails called *lekku*.

123

LEGO minifigures met Japanese manga in the exciting LEGO EXO-FORCE theme. Robot buster Hikaru has a new, angular hair piece made from rubber, and a dual-sided head showing two facial expressions (serious and angry). Both face prints show him wearing an orange visor.

MANGA-INSPIRED HERO!

HIKARU

DON'T MESS THE HAIR!

1 Stylized spiky rubber hair

2 Orange visor printed on head

3 Manga-style features printed on both sides of head

COSTUME CHANGE

A variant Hikaru in a dark blue suit featured in 2007's Sky Guardian (set 8103). He debuted a new white suit in 2008's Chameleon Hunter (set 8114).

POWER BRICKS

Every 2006 LEGO EXO-FORCE set features a light-up brick called a power core.

FIND ME ON THE WEB!

LEGO LEGEND

Spyclops takes his name from the Cyclops, a one-eyed creature from legend.

1 Spider legs attach to neck bracket

2 Frightening face print is part-spider!

3 Just one arm is metallic silver

4 Exclusive printing on mismatched legs

SPYCLOPS

Attention all Ultra Agents! This menacing minifigure is a mash-up of man, machine, and spider! Spyclops has fearsome fangs and two terrifying spider legs sprouting from his back!

ALL LEGS

A similar character called Spy Clops appeared in the LEGO® Agents theme in 2008. He has four eyes and his torso sits on an awesome six-legged spider-leg assembly!

MINI STATS

Theme
LEGO® Ultra Agents

Year
2015

First appearance
Spyclops Infiltration (70166)

Rarity

125

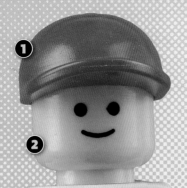

1

2

I'LL NEED TO SEE YOUR ID!

LEGO

Idea House

3

1 Classic peaked cap and original facial expression

2 He's smiling because he knows he's special!

3 LEGO logo and website printed on back of torso

IDEA HOUSE GUY

The Idea House minifigure is available only from the LEGO® Idea House—a special area within the LEGO Group's headquarters in Billund, Denmark. The area is only accessible to LEGO staff and their VIP guests, so you have to be pretty special to get your hands on one.

A CREATIVE SPACE

In 2016, the LEGO Group will open a new LEGO House designed to be an "experience center," where people can learn more about the company and explore their own creativity through LEGO play.

MINI STATS

Theme
LEGO® Space

Year
2009

First appearance
Squidman Escape
(5969)

Rarity

Despite calling himself King of the Squidmen, this alien outlaw is in fact the one and only LEGO squidman! He first busted out in 2009, as part of the Space Police III subtheme, and his bulging, upturned red eyes, fanged mouth, and long tongue make him a very collectible villain!

SCARY SQUID!

SQUIDMAN

NOT GILL-TY, YOUR HONOR!

1 Unusual new head mold

2 Red cape also worn by Superman minifigure

3 Banknote accessory. Stop, thief!

"Squidman got me my job at the LEGO Group! I created him in a hiring workshop in London in 2005. The original design used a LEGO® Technic part as the head. Later, I was able to spend time perfecting it."

TIM AINLEY, LEGO CONCEPT MANAGER SPECIALIST

SQUID ON SCREEN

Squidman can be seen causing trouble in the LEGO DVD movie *The Adventures Of Clutch Powers.*

127

Square-headed Steve is the default player in the construction-centered video game, Minecraft. In this variant, Steve looks ready to defend his resources from the Creepers and the Zombies. For protection, he wears iron armor and a helmet, and carries his trusty pixelated sword!

HE'S A CRAFTY ONE!

MINI STATS

Theme
LEGO® Minecraft™

Year
2014

First appearance
The Mine (21118)

Rarity

STEVE

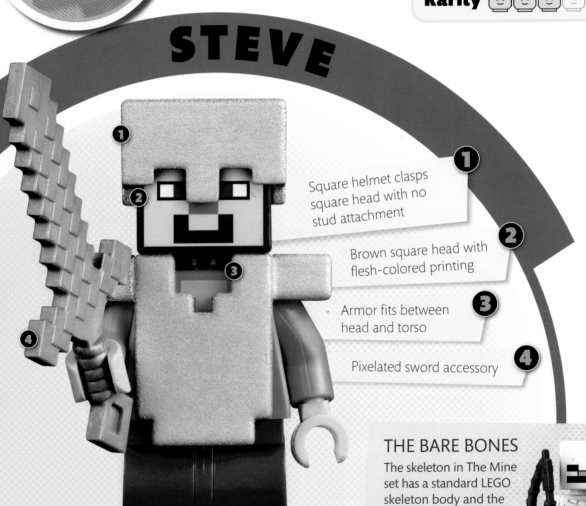

1. Square helmet clasps square head with no stud attachment

2. Brown square head with flesh-colored printing

3. Armor fits between head and torso

4. Pixelated sword accessory

THE BARE BONES

The skeleton in The Mine set has a standard LEGO skeleton body and the same square head mold as Steve, but in white with black and gray printing. It is armed with a bow and arrow.

QUEEN AMIDALA

> IF ONLY YOU KNEW HOW LONG IT TAKES TO PUT ON THIS GET-UP!

1 Unique hair piece with integral gold headdress

2 Exclusive torso print

3 Flesh-colored hands contrast with made-up face

4 Unique skirt with round base piece instead of legs

RIGHT ROYAL RARITY!

Theme
LEGO® Star Wars®

Year
2012

First appearance
Gungan Sub
(9499)

Rarity

SCRATCHED UP!

Another detailed Padmé minifigure is included in the Republic Gunship (set 75021) from 2013. Here, she wears a white top with one sleeve torn off. She also has scratch marks on her back made by a Nexu beast from the Geonosian Arena.

This is the first minifigure to show Padmé Amidala as the Queen of Naboo. It's a faithful reproduction of her outfit in *Star Wars: Episode I The Phantom Menace*, and includes a specially molded headdress. She comes on a unique disc-shaped piece, forming part of the skirt.

I'M A BIG LEGO FAN, DESPITE MY SIZE!

1 Reverse of head has the same grin as Benny from THE LEGO® MOVIE™

2 Balloon print marks ten years of Fan Weekends

3 Back of torso says "LEGO® Fan Weekend 2014"

4 Matching Fan Weekend Guy has blue legs

WHAT A CARD...
A few lucky LEGO Group employees carry minifigures as their business cards!

LEGO Fan Weekends have been held in Skærbæk, Denmark, since 2004, and have seen LEGO fans from all over the world gather to share love for LEGO bricks and minifigures. This happy girl was one of the minifigures produced to mark the tenth Fan Weekend, held in September 2014.

MINI STATS

Theme
N/A

Year
2014

First appearance
LEGO Fan Weekend 2014

Rarity

EARLIER FAN WEEKENDS
The 2009 Fan Weekend minifigure has details of the event printed on the front of his torso. The 2011 version is similar but has darker hair and event details on the back of the torso.

CHAPTER EIGHT
WILD AT HEART

TAKE A WALK ON THE WILD SIDE WITH THESE AMAZING ANIMAL-THEMED CHARACTERS!

The General of the LEGO NINJAGO Anacondrai tribe, Pythor has a long Serpentine tail piece in place of legs. Both this chunky tail and his scary head piece were created especially for him. He may well be the last remaining member of his tribe, but he makes up for it by being the only Serpentine to have a variant: the striking white Pythor released in 2015.

MINI **STATS**

Theme
LEGO® NINJAGO™

Year
2012

First appearance
Ultra Sonic Raider
(9449)

Rarity

THE LAST OF HIS KIND

PYTHOR

JOIN MY FANG CLUB!

OPEN WIDE!
Pythor is the only Serpentine General to have a head with an open mouth.

1 Unique head piece

2 Exclusive printing

3 Most LEGO parts are made from ABS plastic or rubber—this tail piece combines both

HE'S ALL-WHITE!
The 2015 white variant shows Pythor drained of color, apart from purple markings. He appears in Mobile Ninja Base (set 70750).

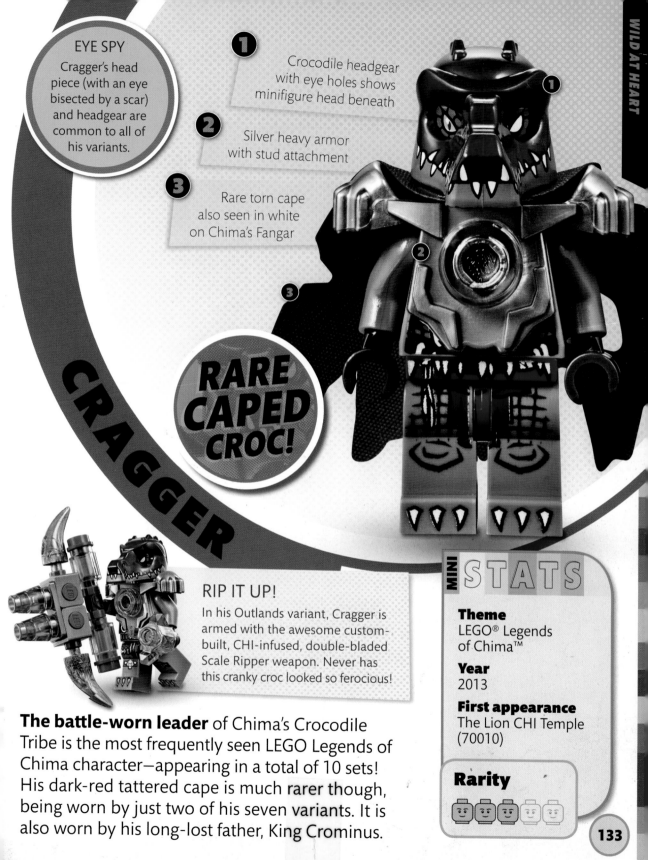

EYE SPY

Cragger's head piece (with an eye bisected by a scar) and headgear are common to all of his variants.

1 Crocodile headgear with eye holes shows minifigure head beneath

2 Silver heavy armor with stud attachment

3 Rare torn cape also seen in white on Chima's Fangar

1

2

3

RARE CAPED CROC!

CRAGGER

RIP IT UP!

In his Outlands variant, Cragger is armed with the awesome custom-built, CHI-infused, double-bladed Scale Ripper weapon. Never has this cranky croc looked so ferocious!

The battle-worn leader of Chima's Crocodile Tribe is the most frequently seen LEGO Legends of Chima character—appearing in a total of 10 sets! His dark-red tattered cape is much rarer though, being worn by just two of his seven variants. It is also worn by his long-lost father, King Crominus.

MINI STATS

Theme
LEGO® Legends of Chima™

Year
2013

First appearance
The Lion CHI Temple (70010)

Rarity

133

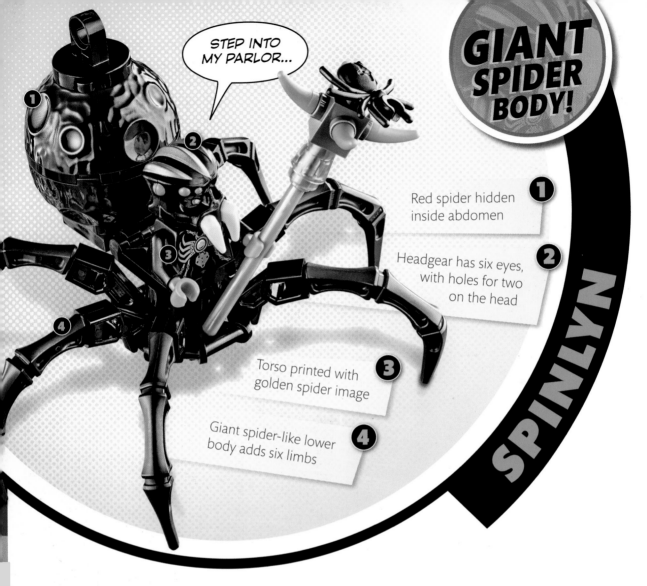

STEP INTO MY PARLOR...

1 Red spider hidden inside abdomen

2 Headgear has six eyes, with holes for two on the head

3 Torso printed with golden spider image

4 Giant spider-like lower body adds six limbs

SPINLYN

MINI STATS

Theme
LEGO® Legends of Chima™

Year
2014

First appearance
Spinlyn's Cavern (70133)

Rarity

The self-styled Queen of the Spider Tribe, Spinlyn is the only Chima minifigure not to have standard legs. The six legs of her spider body and the two arms on her torso give her the necessary total of eight limbs, and make her one of the biggest minifigures of all.

"Using the meteorite piece as her abdomen works really well. You can put baby spiders inside!"

ALEXANDRE BOUDON,
LEGO DESIGN MASTER

This Yeti's new head mold covers most of his torso. Every one of his elements features light royal-blue (except for his fluorescent-blue popsicle), making him only the second Minifigure to use this color—the other being the Scientist from Minifigures Series 11.

KEEPS A COOL HEAD!

 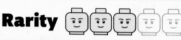

Theme
LEGO® Minifigures

Year
2013

First appearance
LEGO Minifigures
Series 11

Rarity

CLEVER CREATURE
The Yeti is one of the Master Builders seen in THE LEGO® MOVIE™.

YETI

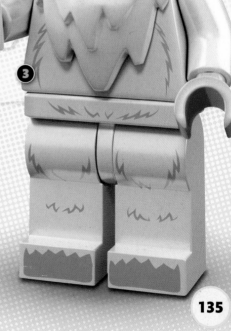

1
New head mold, since used for Breezor the Beaver in LEGO® Legends of Chima™

2
Popsicle seen in more than 30 LEGO sets

3
Light blue printing for shaggy fur effect

ICE TO MEET YOU
The first winter-themed character in the Minifigures theme was the Skier from Series 2. He's easily identifiable out on the slopes, because every part of him (except his hat) is unique.

211

Appearing in just two promotional sets, this minifigure has a unique rabbit mask that fits over the top of a standard-shaped LEGO head. It was designed this way for Quicky's first playset, which features an actor dressing up as the NESQUIK® mascot for a film as part of the LEGO Studios theme. The character's torso design is also exclusive.

QUICKY

Theme
LEGO® Studios

Year
2001

First appearance
Film Set With Quicky
(4049)

Rarity

1 Eye holes show white minifigure head beneath bunny mask

2 Yellow sweater features an "N" for NESQUIK

3 Torso color matches NESQUIK packaging

4 Torso, head, and mask are all exclusive to this minifigure

1

2

3

4

MY FAVORITE ACTOR? I'D HAVE TO SAY RABBIT DE NIRO!

RABBIT RUN
A third set featured Quicky's head peeking out of a race car, but no minifigure body.

RARE RABBIT!

136

TRANSPARENT BLUE BODY PARTS

MAULA

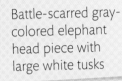

1 Battle-scarred gray-colored elephant head piece with large white tusks

2 Transparent blue armored chestplate

3 Detailed torso print visible beneath transparent piece

4 One transparent blue leg and one gray leg

"I spent a lot of time on Maula's braids and the ornaments on her torso."
TORE HARMARK-ALEXANDERSEN, LEGO DESIGNER

MINI STATS

Theme
LEGO® Legends of Chima™

Year
2014

First appearance
Maula's Ice Mammoth Stomper (70145)

Rarity

This force of nature leads the Mammoth Tribe, and her minifigure looks just as formidable as you'd expect! Maula is unusual because some of her parts are transparent blue, making them look as if they have been carved from ice.

FROZEN FORTRESS

As well as commanding the Ice Mammoth Stomper, Maula also leads her tribe in their impressive but icy base, Mammoth's Frozen Stronghold (set 70226).

HERE KITTY, KITTY, KITTY, KITTY, KITTY, KITTY!

THE CAT'S MEOW!

1 Red glasses frame a concerned expression

2 Unique cat face and fanny-pack print on torso

3 Legs, like torso, are covered in cat hair

4 Comes with a ginger cat accessory

Mrs. Scratchen-Post from THE LEGO MOVIE is Emmet's cat-crazy neighbor. She isn't interested in anything that doesn't look like a cat. It's fortunate her sweater has a cat face on it, or she may never get dressed properly!

A GREAT GRANDMA

Perhaps Mrs. Scratchen-Post is related to the Grandma from LEGO® Minifigures series 11. Grandma has similar glasses and wears a sweater with cat designs on it. Her pet cat is gray.

MINI STATS

Theme
THE LEGO® MOVIE™

Year
2014

First appearance
LEGO Minifigures
The LEGO MOVIE
Series

Rarity

MINI STATS

Theme
THE LEGO® MOVIE™

Year
2014

First appearance
LEGO Minifigures
The LEGO MOVIE
Series

Rarity

Don't be fooled—Panda Guy is more than just a mascot. Lift off the unique head piece and you'll reveal a Master Builder! He is quite an unusual minifigure because he carries a miniature version of the animal he is dressed as!

PANDAS TO YOUR NEEDS!

PANDA GUY

WHAT FOOD SCARES PANDAS?

1 Detachable head piece with eye holes

2 Standard minifigure head beneath is printed with a bead of sweat

3 White printing on black legs (white torso has black printing)

4 Unique panda toy accessory

BAM-BOO!

ANIMAL ATTRACTION

Panda Guy is the sixth minifigure in an animal costume. The others are Gorilla Suit Guy, Lizard Man, Bunny Suit Guy, Chicken Suit Guy, Bumblebee Girl, and Piggy Guy.

There was a buzz when this alien bug winged its way into the LEGO Space subtheme, Galaxy Squad! The Mosquitoid's head is a brand-new mold and it was also the first time this style of wing had been seen on a minifigure.

SWARM FORCE

As well as Mosquitoids, Galaxy Squad also has to contend with Alien Buggoids (both the red and green kind). Where's a giant flyswatter when you need one?

MINI STATS

Theme
LEGO® Space

Year
2013

First appearance
Swarm Interceptor
(70701)

Rarity

WINGED MOSQUITOID

STOP BUGGING ME!

1 New head mold with large compound eyes and pointy proboscis

2 Transparent wings are a single piece and attach at the neck

3 Exoskeleton print on legs and torso

FLY GUY!

TWO HEADS ARE BETTER THAN ONE!

YESSS!

FANGPYRESSS FOREVER!

1

1 Rare, two-headed element

2 Unique scale pattern runs from head to legs

3 Fangdam is the only Fangpyre with red legs

2

3

FANGDAM

Fangdam is the second-in-command of the Fangpyre tribe in the LEGO NINJAGO theme. A Fangpyre's bite can create a new serpent, and Fangdam's second head is the result of a bite from a fellow Fangpyre, who mistook him for a slug!

FAMILY RESEMBLANCE

Fangdam's brother Fangtom has a near identical head piece, with one exception—Fangtom's has white markings on the back, rather than black. His sneaky sibling also has a long tail piece instead of legs.

MINI STATS

Theme
LEGO® NINJAGO™

Year
2012

First appearance
Fangpyre Truck Ambush (9445)

Rarity

GIANT METAL FISTS!

1 Gorilla head over standard minifigure head mold

2 Standard minifigure hands hold giant fist weapons

Fists also seen in the Ultra Agents and NINJAGO™ themes **3**

G'LOONA

LONE WOLF
Like G'Loona, Windra is the only female in her tribe to be made into a minifigure. She appears in just one set to date: Worriz's Combat Lair (set 70009).

G'Loona is the only known female member of Chima's Gorilla Tribe, but what makes her even more special are her huge metal hands. She also has short, unposable legs and a striking costume decorated with pretty pink flowers.

MINI STATS

Theme
LEGO® Minifigures

Year
2013

First appearance
LEGO Minifigures
Series 10

Rarity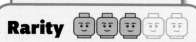

This bee scores an "A" in the collectibility stakes, with unique headgear, unique clear wings, and all-exclusive printing! So far, she is the only female minifigure to dress as an animal, and though she lacks a sting, she has no shortage of honey in her printed pot.

CHOICE OF THE BEEHIVE!

BUMBLEBEE GIRL

A BUSY BEE'S WORK IS NEVER DONE!

1
New cap with insect antennas

2
Plastic wings attach to neck

3
Pot element also carried by Leprechaun minifigure

WINGING IT

Adding a touch of magic to the Series 8 Minifigures, the Fairy wears her wings in transparent blue.

The main bad guy in *The Hobbit* Motion Picture Trilogy, Azog was given out to lucky LEGO fans at San Diego Comic-Con in June 2013. Later that year, he also appeared in a full set, but his Comic-Con release remains highly prized if safely locked away in the original packaging!

BIG BATTLE
Azog's minifigure also appears in Dol Guldur Battle (set 79014).

WHERE'S THE WARG?
In *The Hobbit: An Unexpected Journey*, Azog rides a white warg. One of these appears in LEGO form in Attack of the Wargs (set 79002), but Azog does not.

AZOG

WAIT 'TIL I GET MY CLAW ON THOSE DWARVES!

① Sandwich-board head piece fits over torso

② Metal claw-hand is unique to Azog

③ Fur loincloth printed on torso and leg pieces

④ Weapon made of three pieces

MINI STATS

Theme
LEGO® *The Hobbit*™

Year
2013

First appearance
San Diego Comic-Con 2013 giveaway

Rarity

UNIQUE CLAW HAND!

HOT WINGS!

1 Blazing orange wings

2 Fiery red feathered head piece

3 Gold collar and wing harness, with flame icon

4 Slope piece features belt and pendants

FLUMINOX

PRETTY FLY...
This wing mold was created for the LEGO Legends of Chima theme.

This Phoenix from the LEGO Legends of Chima theme wears an outfit befitting his role as leader of his tribe. He wears new shoulder armor with flame-colored wings attached, and has a unique slope piece printed with ornate golden details.

LEG-ENDS OF CHIMA
Fluminox has a variant with legs instead of a slope piece, so he can sit on his Speedor bike in Inferno Pit (set 70155).

MINI STATS

Theme
LEGO® Legends of Chima™

Year
2014

First appearance
Flying Phoenix Fire Temple (70146)

Rarity

145

1 Exclusive black turtle head piece

2 Printed blue bandana hangs down at back

3 New turtleshell piece attaches with neck bracket

SHADOW LEONARDO

DOWN THE DRAIN

Shadow Leo came mounted on a card designed to look like a sewer cover.

This Ninja Turtle minifigure surfaced at New York Comic-Con in 2012 to introduce the new LEGO Teenage Ninja Turtles theme. Only 300 Shadow Leonardos were produced and all were given away to lucky raffle winners. Each came with a black skateboard that was printed with the event location and date.

GOING GREEN

The first green Leonardo minifigure was released in 2013. Like Shadow Leo, it uses new head and shell molds made especially for the Turtles theme.

MINI STATS

Theme
LEGO® Teenage Mutant Ninja Turtles™

Year
2012

First appeared
New York Comic-Con 2012 giveaway

Rarity

MINI STATS

Theme
LEGO® Minifigures

Year
2013

First appearance
LEGO Minifigures
Series 10

Rarity

A monster straight out of classical myth, Medusa has snakes for hair and even a serpentine tail. Fangs are a recurring theme on her printing, and she has a double-sided head—with each side looking as bad as the other!

SNAKES FOR HAIR!

LEGEND!
Medusa is part of a mythical race of beings called Gorgons.

MEDUSA

LOOK INTO MY EYES...

1 Unique hair piece is alive with snakes!

2 Double-sided head has angry expression on the reverse

3 Green tail piece has flexible rubber tip

TWIST IN THE TAIL
Snake tail pieces were first used for the Serpentine General minifigures in LEGO® NINJAGO™ sets.

Introduced in **2010**, LEGO Atlantis featured many innovative new minifigure designs to form its fierce underwater warriors. A brave Salvage Crew came face to face with all kinds of fishy foes, but none was so memorable as the Squid Warrior and his tentacles of terror!

MINI STATS

Theme
LEGO® Atlantis

Year
2010

First appearance
Gateway of the Squid (8061)

Rarity

TERRIFIC TENTACLES

The terrifying Alien Commander in 2011's LEGO® Alien Conquest sets also used the tentacle piece.

SQUID WARRIOR

SOMETHING SEEMS FISHY TO ME!

1 Unique squid head

2 Eyes printed on head beneath squid piece

3 Gold trident carried by all the underwater warrior minifigures

4 Large tentacle piece in place of standard legs

DEMONS OF THE DEEP

Other unusual undersea creatures encountered by the LEGO Atlantis Salvage Crew include Shark Warriors and Manta Warriors!

LOTS OF LEGS!

CHAPTER NINE
ROTTEN ROGUES

EVEN SOME MINIFIGURES HAVE A DARK SIDE, AND THE ONES IN THIS ROGUES' GALLERY ARE BAD TO THE BASEPLATE!

I AM YOUR MINIFIGURE!

SHINY SITH

1 Gray head under helmet is not painted chrome black

2 Reflective chrome black paint all over

3 Black fabric cape

DARTH VADER (CHROME BLACK)

Just 10,000 of this extra-shiny Sith Lord were produced to mark the 10th anniversary of LEGO *Star Wars*. Coated in chrome black paint, some were randomly included in LEGO *Star Wars* sets, while others were given away at fan events.

MINI STATS

Theme
LEGO® *Star Wars*®

Year
2009

First appearance
Promotional item given away with LEGO *Star Wars* sets

Rarity

DARTH SANTA

The 2014 LEGO *Star Wars* Advent Calendar (set 75056) includes a festive Darth Vader in a red cape and Santa coat, holding a sack of toys for his stormtroopers.

MINI STATS

Theme
LEGO® Agents

Year
2008

First appearance
Volcano Base (8637)

Rarity

We don't know why LEGO Agents villain Claw-Dette replaced her right arm with a claw, but it doesn't seem to have improved her bad mood. The arm is made up of two pieces: a special silver arm piece, created for LEGO Agents, and a gray robot claw hand.

SHE'S GOT A **CLAW** FOR A HAND!

CLAW-DETTE

GET A GRIP!

1 Scary robot claw piece

2 Same face as Evil Witch from LEGO® Castle theme

3 Severe bobbed hairdo

4 Unique torso with Dr. Inferno's logo

SHARE THE HAIR

Nya from LEGO® NINJAGO™ wears the same bob hair piece.

THAT'S HANDY

Dr. Inferno, Claw-Dette's evil boss, also has one robotic claw arm. It must come in useful when styling his incredible hair!

151

This LEGO NINJAGO minifigure is actually two characters in one! On one side of his head piece, he is smiling Cyrus Borg, a skilled inventor. On the other side, he is transformed by technology into the evil villain, OverBorg.

TWO CHARACTERS IN ONE

MINI STATS

Theme
LEGO® NINJAGO™

Year
2014

First appearance
OverBorg Attack (70722)

Rarity

CYRUS BORG

ALLOW ME TO INTRODUCE MY SELVES...

1 Headgear is exclusive to this minifigure

2 OverBorg has a scowl, red eyes, and metallic printing

3 Intricate wire, plate, and pipe printing on unique torso

4 One silver arm and one black arm reflect Borg's two characters

MAN OR MACHINE?
OverBorg's mechanical headgear is part of his hair mold.

TWO-FACED BADDIE

> THERE'S A GOOD COP IN ME... SOMEWHERE!

1 Printed helmet is exclusive to Bad Cop

2 Other side of head shows Good Cop face, with a smile and round glasses

3 Torso print includes badge and walkie-talkie

4 New blaster piece fires trans-red studs

BAD COP

Bad Cop is Lord Business's number one henchman in THE LEGO MOVIE—well, at least one side of his face is! Turn his head around and he becomes kindly Good Cop. This variant is exclusive to the Bad Cop's Pursuit set.

SCRIBBLE FACE

The Scribble Face Bad Cop variant is part of THE LEGO MOVIE Minifigure series. His "Good Cop" face has been rubbed out and drawn back in—badly!

MINI STATS

Theme
THE LEGO® MOVIE™

Year
2014

First appearance
Bad Cop's Pursuit (70802)

Rarity

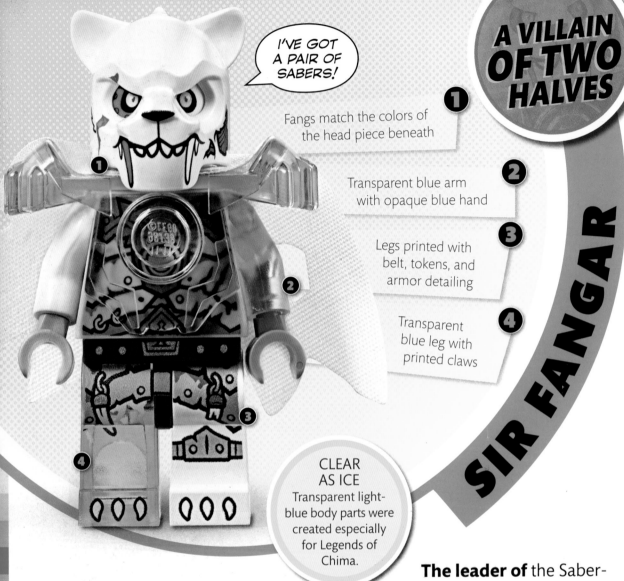

I'VE GOT A PAIR OF SABERS!

A VILLAIN OF TWO HALVES

1 Fangs match the colors of the head piece beneath

2 Transparent blue arm with opaque blue hand

3 Legs printed with belt, tokens, and armor detailing

4 Transparent blue leg with printed claws

SIR FANGAR

CLEAR AS ICE
Transparent light-blue body parts were created especially for Legends of Chima.

The leader of the Saber-Tooth Tiger Tribe, Fangar is a truly fearsome-looking minifigure. He has scars on his face and sharp fangs, but it's his transparent body parts and armor that really make him stand out from the crowd.

MINI STATS

Theme
LEGO® Legends of Chima™

Year
2014

First appearance
Fire vs. Ice (70156)

CAPED CRUSADER
A black version of Sir Fangar's tatty cape is worn by the Batzarro minifigure. This strange clone of Batman is included with the DVD movie LEGO® DC Comics™ Super Heroes: Justice League vs Bizarro League.

MINI STATS

Theme
LEGO® *Star Wars*®

Year
2008

First appearance
Republic Attack
Gunship (7676)

Rarity

This deadly Dathomirian Nightsister made her first appearance in 2008. She comes with cool accessories, including a two unusual lightsabers with curved hilts, and a fabric skirt, which she wears in just one set.

EVIL EYES!

ASAJJ VENTRESS

SO HAVE I!

1 Purple Nightsister tattoos on pale face

2 Unique curved-hilt lightsabers, designed for this minifigure

3 Ventress was the first minifigure to wear a fabric skirt over her legs.

ASAJJ AGAIN

This variant of Ventress appears in the 2011 Sith Nightspeeder (set 7957). She looks quite different, with no cloth skirt and alternative printing on the torso.

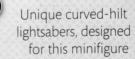

No, this shocking pink vision isn't some wicked creation of the Dark Arts, it's just the Professor Dolores Umbridge minifigure from LEGO Harry Potter! Appearing in one set only, the Professor is really quite rare. Her legs, torso, and head pieces all have unique printing.

VIDEO MAGIC

Professor Umbridge is a playable character in the video game LEGO *Harry Potter: Years 5–7*. She comes armed with a wand.

Theme
LEGO® Harry Potter™

Year
2007

First appearance
Hogwarts Castle (5378)

Rarity

PROFESSOR UMBRIDGE

I WILL HAVE ORDER!

1 Hair piece has been worn by just one other minifigure— in Green Grocer (set 10185)

2 Bright-pink blush on cheeks

3 Torso print shows jacket details and cat brooch

4 Pink suit pants match jacket perfectly!

THINK PINK!

SO SEVERUS!

Also exclusive to Hogwarts Castle is the Severus Snape minifigure. This variant has a black jacket with purple printing on his torso.

ENEMY OF THE AGENTS!

DR. INFERNO

I'M HAIR TO CAUSE TROUBLE!

1 Hair like flames

2 Unique head piece shows mad scientist grin

3 Robot claw later worn by henchwoman, Claw-Dette

4 Stylish suit with flaming skull logo

NO ARM DONE
Before 2008, there had been minifigures with hook-hands, but none had alternative arm pieces.

MINI STATS

Theme
LEGO® Agents

Year
2008

First appearance
Mobile Command Center (8635)

Rarity

This evil genius on the LEGO Agents' most-wanted list soon joined LEGO fans' most-wanted lists, too. With a striking new hair piece and a robotic claw, Dr. Inferno is particularly notable for being the first LEGO minifigure with a non-standard arm.

A KNIGHT'S TALE
The very first minifigure villain charged into action 30 years before Dr. Inferno. The Black Cavalry Knight was included in Castle (set 375). His smiling face was hidden by a black visor.

I'M REALLY ADVANCED!

SHADOW ARF TROOPER

1 Silver printed visor

2 Standard clone head under helmet

3 Armor printing in exclusive color scheme

4 Black hips and hands common to all ARF Troopers

NOT ARF!

The Shadow ARF Trooper doesn't appear in any films—he only appears in the LEGO *Star Wars* galaxy.

MINI STATS

Theme
LEGO® *Star Wars*®

Year
2011

First appearance
May the 4th promotional giveaway

Rarity

The Shadow ARF Trooper was given away exclusively as a *Star Wars* "May the Fourth be With You" promotional item in 2011. With black legs, helmet, and torso, this minifigure can disappear easily into the shadows—just don't let it disappear from your collection!

HOW THE OTHER ARF LIVE

ARF (Advanced Recon Force) Troopers are clones that carry out reconnaissance missions. Most wear white armor, so the Shadow variant is extra stealthy!

MINI STATS

Theme
LEGO® *Indiana Jones*™

Year
2009

First appearance
The Temple of Doom
(7199)

Rarity

The terrifying high priest Mola Ram is leader of the Thuggee cult in *Indiana Jones and the Temple of Doom*. He's an intimidating villain who strikes fear into his enemies with his scary horned headdress. It's lucky for Indy and his pals that he appears in only one set!

THIS RAM HAS HORNS!

MOLA RAM

1. Unique headdress with detachable horns

2. Exclusive head with red facepaint under headdress

3. Unique torso design depicts tooth necklace

PARDON?

LOOK CLOSER...
The small brown head on Mola Ram's headdress looks very worried. Who wouldn't be?

WORN HORNS

Mola Ram's detachable horns also appear on the Minotaur, part of the sixth series of collectible Minifigures from 2012.

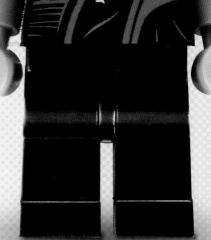

159

This **2012 variant** of Gotham's most wanted eco-warrior is notable for the decorative vine trail that covers much of her torso and the top half of her legs. Her distinctive red hair piece was introduced with the minifigure and has five green leaves printed on the front.

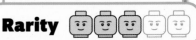

NOTORIOUS
BATMAN VILLAIN

MINI **STATS**

Theme
LEGO® DC Comics™
Super Heroes

Years
2012–2013, 2015

First appearance
The Batcave
(6860)

Rarity

POISON IVY

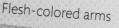

I'M ALL FOR GOING GREEN!

1 Green leaves printed on red hair piece

2 Distinctive thick eyelashes and dark green lipstick

3 Winding vine trail runs from torso to leg pieces

4 Flesh-colored arms

VINE BY ME!
Both the 2006 and the 2012 Poison Ivy minifigures come with green vine accessories.

DARKER SIDE

The original Poison Ivy minifigure is based on the character from *Batman: The Animated Series* and has darker hair than the 2012 variant, as well as a brighter shade of green lipstick.

HE'S ALL WHITE!

① Plain black head piece shows through helmet

② Helmet and jetpack are all one piece

③ No printing except simple torso design

FETT OF THE FAIR

White Boba Fett was first seen at the 2010 Canadian Toy Fair, where he was given out to 150 lucky fans!

BOBA FETT (WHITE)

BATTLE-SCARRED

Another variant of Boba was released in 2010 as part of *Slave I* (set 8097). He has a battle-damaged helmet, a separate jetpack, a scarred head, a ragged brown cape over one shoulder, and a blaster extended with a LEGO® Technic piece.

Based on early *Star Wars* concept art from the 1970s, this striking white Boba Fett was given away to celebrate the 30th anniversary of *The Empire Strikes Back*. Only 10,000 were made, making this Boba a much-hunted bounty hunter!

MINI STATS

Theme
LEGO® *Star Wars*®

Year
2010

First appearance
Star Wars: The Empire Strikes Back 30th anniversary promotional minifigure

Rarity

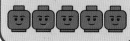

161

FIRST REVERSE HEAD!

① Purple turban is a first for a minifigure

② Double-sided head piece with Voldemort's face printed on the reverse

③ Torso shows purple jacket and matching scarf

④ Black fabric cape

I'M HIDING A TERRIBLE SECRET!

MINI STATS

Theme
LEGO® Harry Potter™

Year
2001

First appearance
The Final Challenge (4702)

Rarity

BACK IN BLACK

Professor Quirrell's minifigure marked the first appearance of Lord Voldemort in LEGO Harry Potter. The final version (shown here) was released in 2010 in Hogwarts Castle (set 4842), and The Forbidden Forest (set 4865) the following year.

Who's that hiding under Professor Quirinus Quirrell's turban? Why, it's only you-know-who, Lord Voldemort! This minifigure was the first to have a double-sided head, featuring Quirrell's face on one side and Lord Voldemort's on the other. No collector can quarrel with Quirrell!

MINI  STATS

Theme
LEGO® City

Year
2013

First appearance
LEGO City Starter Set
(60023)

Rarity

STOP, THIEF!

LEGO City has seen its fair share of bad guys over the years, but even its biggest villains have a loveable look! This classic Crook has a stylish mustache and wears the (not-so-stylish) striped shirt of an escaped prisoner.

CROOK

WHO WAS THAT MASKED MAN?
Ten other minifigures have this masked face print, which must make police ID parades very difficult!

CATCH ME IF YOU CAN!

1 Dark tan sack also used by four Santa minifigure variants!

2 Many LEGO City crooks carry this red crowbar

3 Prison fatigues torso print first seen in 2005

BEARDY BADDIE
This bearded bad guy is new for 2015's LEGO City Swamp Police subtheme. He has a brand new beard piece that fits between his head and torso.

Kitted out all in black, the original Blacktron Spaceman is light years ahead of the classic LEGO® astronauts that preceded him. Don't let his smile fool you, though—these stylish rocketeers were the first LEGOLAND Space bad guys, traveling the galaxy purely for profit.

FIRST SPACE VILLAIN

MINI STATS

Theme
LEGOLAND® Space
Years
1987–1991, 2009
First appearance
Meteor Monitor (1875)

Rarity

BLACKTRON SPACEMAN

TO INFINITE MONEY AND BEYOND!

1 LEGOLAND Space helmet with opaque visor new for 1987

2 Neck bracket secures black airtank

3 Torso also seen on the Octan Mag Racer minifigure from 1992

NUMBER ONE FAN
The Blacktron Spaceman has a not-so-secret admirer: Blacktron Fan. He can be seen in THE LEGO® MOVIE™ as Emmet lists all the awesome things about the Octan Corporation.

MINI STATS

Theme
LEGO® Teenage
Mutant Ninja Turtles™

Year
2012

First appearance
The Kraang Rockefeller
Center LEGO Store
Promotional Set

Rarity

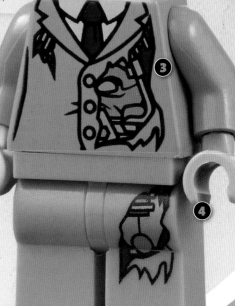

❶ Jet-black, side-parted hair piece

❷ Damaged human features reveal robotic head beneath

❸ Green-eyed Kraang can be seen through a tear in the suit

❹ One gray robot hand

KRAANG (DAMAGED)

This exclusive
Teenage Mutant Ninja
Turtles minifigure was created
for an event at the Rockefeller Center
LEGO Store in New York. Given away to
customers dressed as Turtles,
it depicts one of the
blobby alien baddies
in a damaged robot-
human body, its
true form visible
through tears in
the character's suit.

YOU KRAANG?

A "Kraangdroid" robot that makes no attempt to look human appears in three LEGO Teenage Mutant Ninja Turtle sets. It has a gray jetpack and a torso print that shows the Kraang alien in all its glory!

I'M STEALING GOLD TO PAY FOR A SHAVE!

HAT'S AMAZING!
All three hats in the Black Seas Barracuda set were brand new designs—including one worn by the ship's masthead!

1 Three-cornered or "tricorn" hat

2 Printed eyepatch new for 1989

3 Printed stubble and shaggy hair

4 Five variants wear this torso print

MINI STATS

Theme
LEGO® Pirates

Years
1989, 2002

First appearance
Black Seas Barracuda (6285)

Rarity

This pirate has the recognizable cheery smile of a minifigure, but also the scruffy hair, eyepatch, and stubble of a scoundrel! This added detail, and his new tricorn hat and torso, were all part of a new kind of minifigure, introduced in the LEGO Pirates theme in 1989.

IS HAT A FACT?
LEGO headgear has been around even longer than the modern minifigure. The first LEGO figures, released in 1975, wore them despite not having faces or hands to put them on with!

LOOK AT HIS NEW HAT!

CHAPTER TEN
WE HAVE THE POWER!

AS IF IT WASN'T ENOUGH FUN BEING A LEGO® MINIFIGURE, THESE HEROES AND VILLAINS HAVE SUPER POWERS AS WELL!

CURSE YOU, CELLPHONES! I'VE NOWHERE TO CHANGE ANY MORE!

DARK KENT!

SUPERMAN (BLACK SUIT)

1 Hair piece with curl unique to Superman minifigures

2 Same face print as Man of Steel variant

3 Monochrome version of Man of Steel torso design

4 Black fabric cape

BACK IN BLACK
Superman first wore a black suit in issue 25 of the *Man of Steel* comic.

MINI STATS

Theme
LEGO® DC Comics™ Super Heroes

Year
2013

First appearance
San Diego Comic-Con 2013 giveaway

Rarity

This event-exclusive version of Superman was given to raffle winners at the 2013 San Diego Comic-Con. Presented in a blister pack on a card backing board, he resembles the Man of Steel variant, but in much darker tones.

TAKE A BOW (AND ARROW)
A Green Arrow minifigure was also exclusively designed for San Diego Comic-Con 2013. He is styled after the New 52 DC Comics series.

MINI STATS

Theme
LEGO® NINJAGO™

Year
2015

First appearance
Condrai Copter
Attack (70746)

Rarity

Five brave ninja protect the LEGO NINJAGO world—dressed in black, red, blue, white, and green. But in 2015, fans were introduced to a mysterious sixth ninja, dressed all in orange. Only time would tell whether this colorful newcomer would join forces with the five ninja boys or fight against them!

ONLY ORANGE NINJA

SKYLOR

NAME THE FLAME
Skylor's outfit color is known as "flame yellowish orange" on the LEGO color palette.

ORANGE IS THE NEW BLACK!

1 Printing shows Japanese symbol for the number six

2 Other side of head is printed with scary white eyes

3 Skylor is the only NINJAGO ninja with a quiver of arrows

BAD DAD
Skylor's father is the villainous Master Chen. His minifigure has a unique headdress and appears in two sets: Condrai Copter Attack and Enter The Serpent (set 70749).

169

Made for the LEGO *Star Wars* Clone Wars™ subtheme, this minifigure of the Mirialan Jedi Knight Barriss Offee comes with a short cape usually worn by smaller minifigures. The cape is an unusual dark-blue color and has a matching molded-plastic hood.

RARE SHORT, DARK-BLUE CAPE

MINI STATS

Theme
LEGO® *Star Wars*®

Year
2012

First appearance
Geonosian Cannon
(9491)

Rarity

BARRISS OFFEE

1 Facial tattoos are printed on the rare light green-colored head piece

2 Torso is printed on the front only

3 Printed details show the Jedi Padawan's unique outfit

4 Blue-bladed lightsaber with silver hilt

ANOTHER CUT OF OFFEE

The Barriss Offee minifigure from 2010 has a longer black cape and hood piece, as well as smaller eyes and different tattoos than the more stylized Clone Wars version.

BUTT-COVERING CLOAK!

VITRUVIUS

I LIKED ME BEFORE I WAS COOL!

1 Comes with an impressive staff—or a chewed-up lollipop!

2 Headband is part of hair piece, but beard is separate

3 Vitruvius is the only non-licensed minifigure with flesh-colored skin

4 Groovy tie-dyed T-shirt beneath robe

MINI STATS

Theme
THE LEGO® MOVIE™

Year
2014

First appearance
Lord Business' Evil Lair (70809)

Rarity

This LEGO MOVIE minifigure is only available in two sets. But what makes Vitruvius really special is his specially molded knotted beard piece and his sparkly blue cloak, both of which are unique to his character.

HAUNTINGLY FAMILIAR

The ghost version of Vitruvius uses a variation of the classic LEGO Ghost from 1990, but with Vitruvius' characteristic headband added. The torso is plain white and the head is black.

171

WELL, WELL, WELL! LOOK WHAT WE HAVE HERE!

BELLATRIX LESTRANGE

1 Long, curly hair piece is unique to this minifigure

2 Double-sided head piece, with a smiling face on one side and a worried expression on the other

3 Silver and blue details are printed on the torso and skirt

4 Printing continues on the back

With her luxurious and curly black locks, Bellatrix Lestrange's LEGO Harry Potter minifigure looks like someone worked a hair-thickening charm on it! Lord Voldemort's loyal follower was brought to life in 2010, and is exclusive to just one set.

MINI STATS

Theme
LEGO® Harry Potter™

Year
2010

First appearance
The Burrow (4840)

Rarity

WHICH WITCH?

Witches aren't confined to the world of Harry Potter! The second series of collectible Minifigures includes a wicked-looking Witch, whose skin is a shade of green not shared by anyone else in the theme.

MINI STATS

Theme
LEGO® DC Comics™
Super Heroes

Year
2011

First appearance
San Diego Comic-Con
2011 giveaway

Rarity

HOLD THE FRONT PAGE!

A second wave of Green Lanterns was given away at the New York Comic-Con in 2011, but now on a Big Apple-themed backing card.

Presented to winning ticket holders at the 2011 San Diego Comic-Con, this minifigure was created to celebrate the launch of the LEGO DC Comics theme. Only a few thousand were made, and they came mounted on cards printed to look like a San Diego newspaper.

GREEN LANTERN

PEOPLE ALWAYS TAKE A SHINE TO ME!

1 Hair piece also seen on the Mutt Williams minifigure from LEGO® *Indiana Jones*™

2 Double-sided head piece also features an angry expression

3 Lantern Corps symbol on torso

NEVER SEEN IN STORES

A LARGER LANTERN
A LEGO Ultrabuild version of Green Lantern was released in 2012.

173

The ninth variant of Zane to be released is the first to expose his robotic inner workings! Showing why the Ninja of Ice is so cool, this minifigure features all exclusive printing plus metallic silver detailing, and is exclusive to just one NINJAGO set.

ROBOT IN DISGUISE

Battle-damaged Zane is a variation on the Rebooted Zane minifigure, found only in Destructoid (set 70726), from 2014.

MINI STATS

Theme
LEGO® NINJAGO™

Year
2014

First appearance
NinjaCopter
(70724)

Rarity

ZANE (BATTLE-DAMAGED)

ZANE AGAIN!
Zane has more variants than any other NINJAGO minifigure.

HEAVY METAL? I'M MORE INTO COOL JAZZ!

1 Hair piece also worn by Agent Swift in LEGO® Ultra Agents

2 Unique face print reveals the robot workings inside Zane's head

3 Torso print continues on back with Ice Dragon logo on tattered robe

4 Mismatched 'titanium' arm

AN ICY LOOK!

SEA LEGS

The Rescue from the Merpeople set includes a merperson minifigure with a fish tail piece instead of legs.

HAPPY SNAPPER

I AM A CHAMPION!

VIKTOR KRUM

1 Unique shark's head element fits over standard minifigure head

2 Beneath shark piece, standard head is printed with Viktor's normal face

3 Torso shows Durmstrang crest

4 Red hips for swimming trunks

In the Triwizard Tournament, Viktor Krum must compete against fellow wizard Harry Potter. Ready for an underwater task, Krum transforms his head into that of a shark! No other minifigure has this shark piece, which can be removed to reveal his normal face.

SHIP SHAPE

In 2005's The Durmstrang Ship (set 4768), the Viktor Krum minifigure wears his gray Durmstrang uniform with printed fur collar and spiky buttons. He has a large, furry hat and stubble printed on his face.

MINI STATS

Theme
LEGO® Harry Potter™

Year
2005

First apperance
Rescue from the Merpeople (4762)

Rarity

175

I'M AFRAID YOU'RE IN FOR A SHOCK!

1 Same combed-back hair piece as fellow good guy Bruce Wayne

2 Unique face print includes open-mouthed version on reverse

3 Exclusive torso print shows cape chain and muscle tone

4 White fabric cape also worn by Mon Mothma and Princess Leia in LEGO® Star Wars®

SHAZAM

HIDDEN HERO

Shazam is an unlockable character in some versions of the video game LEGO® Batman™ 2.

Made especially for the 2012 San Diego Comic-Con, where a limited number were given away to very lucky raffle winners, this LEGO DC Comics Shazam minifigure is highly prized among LEGO collectors. He came presented on a colorful card mount, designed to look like a comic-book cover.

CON MEN

Shazam wasn't the only LEGO DC Comics character up for grabs at Comic-Con 2012. Superman's mixed-up clone, Bizarro, also got the exclusive minifigure treatment.

MINI STATS

Theme
LEGO® DC Comics™ Super Heroes

Year
2012

First appearance
San Diego Comic-Con 2012 giveaway

Rarity

MINI STATS

Theme
LEGO® NINJAGO™

Year
2014

First appearance
Nindroid MechDragon
(70725)

Rarity

The first four Sensei Wu minifigures all had the same white beard and a wise expression. But that all changed in 2013, when the character got an evil tech overhaul! This new Wu is found in just one NINJAGO set and remains the only variant to have a black beard and a silver hat.

HATS OFF!
Wu was the first minifigure to wear a conical hat.

SENSEI OOH!

EVIL WU

DESTROY... ALL... NINJA!

1 Wu's silver hat appears in just one other set—as part of a train!

2 Wu's cyborg implants are the sssinister work of Pythor

3 All Wu variants have a short white beard printed beneath the molded beard—even this one!

4 Beard element fits between minifigure head and torso

WU'S A PRETTY BOY

Happily, Wu became good again, and turned up with his usual white beard, and exclusive printing, in the DK book LEGO® NINJAGO™ *Secret World of the Ninja*.

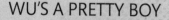

GOLDEN HAIR

Also known as the Lady of Lórien, Galadriel is one of three exclusive minifigures in the Witch-King Battle set, alongside a new variant of Elrond of Rivendell, and the terrifying glow-in-the-dark Witch-King himself! She has all-new printing and a golden hair piece.

MINI **STATS**

Theme
LEGO® *The Hobbit*™

Year
2014

First appearance
Witch-King Battle (79015)

Rarity

GALADRIEL

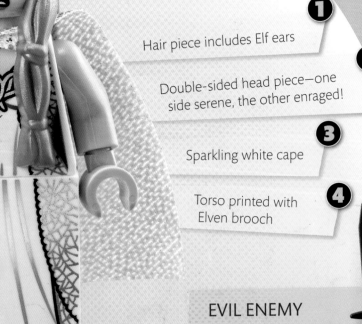

THOU SHALL FEEL MY WRATH, MINIONS OF SAURON!

ELVISH LOOKALIKE
Elrond of Rivendell has the same Elvish hair as Galadriel, but in a dark brown color.

1 Hair piece includes Elf ears

2 Double-sided head piece—one side serene, the other enraged!

3 Sparkling white cape

4 Torso printed with Elven brooch

EVIL ENEMY
The Witch-King minifigure is one scary guy! As well as glowing in the dark, he also wears a creepy spiked crown!

DARTH MAUL

I WILL START WITH REVENGE... AND END AS A MINIFIGURE

1 Horned Zabrak head piece can be swapped for molded hood element

2 New face print also used for "Santa Maul" in 2012 LEGO *Star Wars* Advent Calendar

3 Double-bladed lightsaber with chrome hilt

NEW HORNS!

MINI STATS

Theme
LEGO® *Star Wars*®

Year
2011

First appearance
Darth Maul's Sith Infiltrator (7961)

Rarity

After two hooded variants, this was the first Maul minifigure to show his Zabrak horns, thanks to a new piece that crowns his standard head mold. A hood piece was still included though, as befits a secretive Sith.

YOU'VE GOT MAUL
A hooded Darth Maul features in the very first LEGO *Star Wars* set: Lightsaber Duel (set 7101) from 1999.

SITH ROBOT
Mandalorian Speeder (set 75022) includes a cyborg Darth Maul with unique robot legs and rare printed arms.

ZEN EXTREME NINJA

COLE ZX

I FEEL PRETTY ZEN!

1 Silver crest on cowl denotes Cole's ZX status

2 Shoulder armor includes slots for two swords

3 Lightweight armor printing

4 Back of torso shows golden Earth Dragon symbol

SHOULDER TO SHOULDER

Cole's pauldrons can also be seen on the evil scientist Baxter, from LEGO® Teenage Mutant Ninja Turtles™.

MINI STATS

Theme
LEGO® NINJAGO™

Year
2012

First appearance
Cole's Tread Assault (9444)

Rarity

Cole ZX is the third variant of the Ninja of Earth. He is back in black, but this time he is "shouldering" heavy-duty armor. These daunting-looking pauldrons have function as well as style—they can hold a pair of katanas across Cole's back. Looks like he means business!

KENDO ATTITUDE

ZX isn't the only Cole minifigure with body armor. Cole (Kendo) has a protective plate covering his front and back torso, as well as a mask with a white grille. En garde!

MINI STATS

Theme
LEGO® *Star Wars*®

Year
2005

First appearance
Clone Turbo Tank (7261)

Rarity

This is one minifigure that really puts the "light" into lightsaber! A battery in the torso powers an LED in the lightsaber hilt, illuminating the purple blade when a button on the head is pressed. That's the power of the light side!

LIGHTSABER LIGHTS UP!

RARE WEAPON

When the Clone Turbo Tank set was re-released, it came without light-up elements.

MACE WINDU

LET THE FORCE LIGHT YOUR WAY!

1 Top of head is a button that turns the light on and off

2 Cape, head, and torso cannot be separated

3 Lightsaber is fixed to special arm piece

4 No other Jedi has a purple lightsaber

ILLUMINATED LUMINARA

Luminara Unduli is another minifigure released with a light-up lightsaber. Exclusive to Wookiee Catamaran (set 7260), she comes with an exclusive headdress and a black cape.

The **2013 version** of the NINJAGO super-baddie is more terrifying than ever! As well as his extra torso piece that gives him added height (and arms!), he comes equipped with the horrifying Helmet of Shadows—made up of three LEGO pieces.

FOUR-ARMED FOE!

MINI STATS

Theme
LEGO® NINJAGO™

Year
2013

First appearance
Temple Of Light (70505)

Rarity

LORD GARMADON

WELL ARMED

The LEGO® Teenage Mutant Ninja Turtles™ Robo Foot Ninja also has a torso extender.

I SHALL DESTROY THE NINJA ONCE AND FOR ALL!

1 Clip-on horns also used on staff

2 Bat-like wings are part of a detachable visor that clips on to samurai helmet

3 Torso extender also worn by Lord Garmadon in two 2012 sets

4 Torso extender covers ribcage print on torso

BACK TO HIS SENSEI

The Sensei Garmadon minifigure from 2014 marks Garmadon's move away from villainy with a new, non-evil look.

CHAPTER ELEVEN

ALL-TIME ICONS

WHEN IT COMES TO THE FAME GAME, THERE'S NOTHING "MINI" ABOUT ANY OF THESE GREAT MINIFIGURES!

THAT DOCTOR JONES LOOKS FAMILIAR...

PRINCESS LEIA

1 Only Leia wears this iconic "cinnamon bun" hairstyle

2 Face print also used for Mon Mothma minifigure

3 2011 variant has the same torso, but a new face and hair piece

4 The 2000 variant is identical, except for yellow hands and head

SUPER-SIZED SET

The only set with more pieces than the Ultimate Collector's *Millennium Falcon* is the Taj Mahal (set 10189), with 5,922 pieces.

This highly prized Princess was first seen in the vast Ultimate Collector's *Millennium Falcon* set—amid a total of 5,195 LEGO elements! She went on to appear in two other sought-after sets: the Death Star (set 10188) and *Tantive IV* (set 10198).

HOTH LEIA

The only other version of Princess Leia to wear her hair in buns is dressed for the icy planet Hoth, and comes in yellow and flesh-colored variants.

MINI STATS

Theme
LEGO® *Star Wars*®

Years
2007–2009

First appearance
Ultimate Collector's *Millennium Falcon* (10179)

Rarity

MINI STATS

Theme
LEGO® Indiana Jones™

Years
2008–2009

First appearance
Temple Escape (7623)

Rarity

In 2008, *Indiana Jones and the Kingdom of the Crystal Skull* saw actor Harrison Ford return to the big screen as the whip-cracking adventurer. That same year, Indy made his debut as a LEGO minifigure!

FORTUNE AND GLORY!

EVER-PRESENT
Every set in the LEGO *Indiana Jones* theme features a minifigure of Indy!

INDIANA JONES

I SHOULD BE IN A MUSEUM!

1 Fedora hat designed for LEGO *Indiana Jones* theme

2 Flexible whip

3 Shoulder bag can be removed

4 Leg piece features printed gun holster

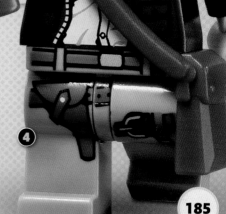

1

2

3

4

DOCTORS JONES
Variants of Indy include: Indy in a gray suit; Indy without his jacket; grinning Indy; and Indy in a dapper white tuxedo!

One of the few yellow Lukes not to have been reissued in a flesh-colored variant, this minifigure depicts the Jedi in training under Master Yoda on the jungle planet Dagobah. It is one of only two Luke variants with bare arms—the other being the "bacta tank" variant found in Hoth Echo Base (set 7879).

REBEL YELLOW!

MINI STATS

Theme
LEGO® *Star Wars*®

Year
2004

First appearance
X-Wing Fighter (4502)

Rarity

LUKE SKYWALKER (DAGOBAH)

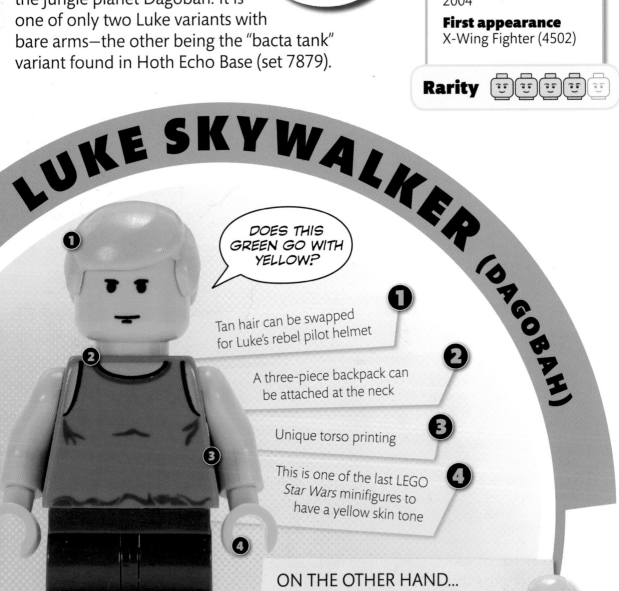

DOES THIS GREEN GO WITH YELLOW?

1 Tan hair can be swapped for Luke's rebel pilot helmet

2 A three-piece backpack can be attached at the neck

3 Unique torso printing

4 This is one of the last LEGO *Star Wars* minifigures to have a yellow skin tone

ON THE OTHER HAND...

There are 11 Luke Skywalker variants with yellow heads, but only seven have all yellow hands! Two wear black pilot's gloves, while those in Speeder Bikes (set 7128) and Final Duel II (set 7201) each have one yellow hand and one black "cybernetic" hand.

HARRY POTTER (BLACK COAT)

> I SOLEMNLY SWEAR THAT I'M VERY GOOD!

1 Every Harry has this hair piece—except for one in a sorting hat

2 Double-sided face print shows frown on other side

3 Formal robes for Slug Club Christmas party

4 This is the only Harry with printed legs

THE **LAST** WIZARD

IN DISGUISE

In Slytherin (set 4735) from 2002, Harry is disguised as Gregory Goyle! Dressed in Hogwarts uniform with the Slytherin crest on the torso, he has Goyle's face printed on one side of his head and Harry's face on the other.

Exclusive to the DK book LEGO® Harry Potter™: *Characters of the Magical World*, this Harry variant has the distinction of being the final minifigure in the Harry Potter theme to date, arriving in stores one year after the last two play sets.

MINI **STATS**

Theme
LEGO® Harry Potter™

Year
2012

First appearance
DK's LEGO Harry Potter: *Characters of the Magical World* book

Rarity

TO THE MYSTERY MACHINE!

1. Unique hair piece has a stylized cartoon shape

2. Scared face on reverse

3. Two-piece camera accessory

4. Printing continues on to side of legs

VELMA DINKLEY

SHE'S A SCOOBY STAR!

MINI STATS

Theme
LEGO® Scooby-Doo™

Year
2015

First appearance
Mystery Mansion (75904)

Rarity

Unmasked in 2015 as part of the new Scooby-Doo theme, Velma sets out to solve spooky mysteries with her friends Shaggy, Fred, and Daphne—with help from Shaggy's dog, Scooby, of course! Velma features in just one of the five Scooby-Doo sets released to date.

MAN OF MYSTERY

Velma's friend Fred carries a working magnifier and a clue to a mystery! He appears only in The Mystery Machine (set 75902).

MINI STATS

Theme
LEGO® Star Wars®

Year
2010

First appearance
Exclusive promotional giveaway

Rarity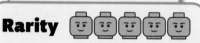

Two—that's right, just two—solid bronze Boba Fett minifigures were ever made. Both were given away during the LEGO *Star Wars* May the 4th promotion in 2010, making this bounty hunter rarer than an honest trader at the Mos Eisley spaceport!

CAST IN SOLID BRONZE

BOBA FETT (BRONZE)

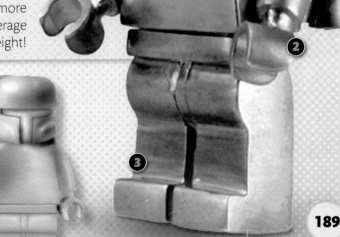

EVEN I COULDN'T HUNT ONE OF THESE DOWN!

1 Bronze Boba has all the molded detail of the original, but none of the printing

2 Torso, legs, head, and helmet are still four separate elements

3 Stands firm at more than three times average minifigure weight!

PRECIOUS METAL

Two 14-carat gold and two sterling silver Boba Fetts were also made in 2010. They were presented, along with a white Boba and a certificate, in two frames, and given to a pair of lucky fans at San Diego Comic-Con and *Star Wars* Celebration V.

The **LEGO** *Collector's Guide* *Premium Edition* is an 800-page book that details almost every LEGO set ever made. The special hardback edition was limited to just 3,333 copies, and came with two exclusive bricks with "LEGO® fan" and "1958–2008" printed on them—and this smiley and highly sought-after commemorative minifigure!

HAPPY BIRTHDAY BOY!

MINI STATS

Theme
N/A

Year
2008

First appearance
LEGO® *Collector's Guide Premium Edition* (810004)

Rarity

50TH ANNIVERSARY GUY

WHERE'S MY WALKING STICK?

1 Red peaked cap piece

2 Face print has a timeless smile for all occasions!

3 Glittery torso print marks the golden anniversary of the LEGO brick

SAY HELLO TO BOB!

Something of a LEGO mascot, Bob is a simple minifigure who appears in several places on LEGO.com and other LEGO Group materials. He features as a physical minifigure in some editions of the Large Minifigure Display Case (set 752437).

PETER VENKMAN

1 NINJAGO™ character Griffin Turner also has this hair piece.

2 Exclusive face print shows a terrified look on the other side!

3 All four Ghostbusters have unique torsos with their initials on the front.

4 Proton pack built with 13 elements including neck bracket

I FEEL SO FUNKY!

WHO YA GONNA CALL?

Busting out of the LEGO Ideas program that sees fan-builds become real LEGO sets, the Ecto-1 set features all four Ghostbusters in minifigure form. Based on an idea by Brent Waller, it was released in time for the 30th anniversary of *Ghostbusters* in 2014.

GHOSTBUSTERS FOUR

All four Ghostbusters appear in the Ecto-1 set: Peter Venkman, Egon Spengler, Ray Stantz, and Winston Zeddemore. Each has his own proton pack and scared face print.

MINI STATS

Theme
LEGO® Ideas

Year
2014

First appearance
Ghostbusters
Ecto-1 (21108)

Rarity

SORRY! I DON'T WANT ANY ADVENTURES, THANK YOU

1 Same hair piece as fellow Hobbit, Samwise Gamgee

2 Double-sided face print with worried expression on reverse

3 Exclusive torso print creates the effect of high pants

4 All Hobbit minifigures have short legs

LEGO fans who followed a map of "ComicCondor" at the 2012 San Diego Comic-Con were the first to get their hands on this minifigure, along with a woven bag in which to keep him. He has since appeared in a regular set, but remains precious with the bag and map.

MINI STATS

Theme
LEGO® The Hobbit™

Year
2012

First appearance
San Diego Comic-Con
2012 giveaway

Rarity

A HANDFUL OF HOBBITS

There are four other Bilbo Baggins variants, including one in checkered pajamas that was exclusive to pre-orders of LEGO® The Hobbit™: The Video Game, and one in a dark blue jacket, found only in The Lonely Mountain (set 79018).

MINI STATS

Theme
THE LEGO® MOVIE™

Year
2014

First appearance
MetalBeard's Sea Cow
(70810)

Rarity

Benny is the first minifigure that is meant to look broken. His helmet is molded to seem snapped at the chin, because he is based on the first LEGOLAND® Space explorers from the 1970s and 1980s, whose helmets were not as strong as the ones worn by minifigures today. His torso design is also deliberately aged and worn away.

HE'S A SNAPPED ACTOR!

BENNY

MOVIE STARMAN

Benny is one of the stars of THE LEGO® MOVIE™, in which Vitruvius calls him "1980-something space guy".

> HI, I'M BENNY! GLAD TO MEET... SPACESHIP!

1 Helmet is not really cracked

2 Double-sided face printing has traditional minifigure face on the reverse

3 Oxygen pack design is unchanged since the 1970s

4 Classic LEGO Space logo is aged to look well played-with

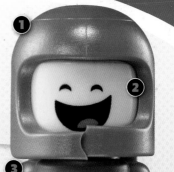

COSMIC KIN

The first blue LEGO spaceman appeared as the pilot of Space Dart-I (set 6824) in 1984. He featured in a total of 12 sets.

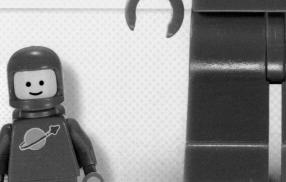

While Gandalf the Grey casts his spell over seven sets, Gandalf the White is exclusive to just one, and has no parts in common with his predecessor. New face and torso printing is only partly obscured by his all-in-one majestic flowing hair and beard element!

WHAT A WIZARD!

MINI STATS

Theme
LEGO® *The Lord of the Rings*™

Year
2013

First appearance
Battle at the Black Gate (79007)

Rarity

GANDALF THE WHITE

I HAVE RETURNED...

1 Long hair and beard are one element

2 Different face print from "Gandalf the Grey" variant

3 Gandalf's white cape is also worn by his enemy— the evil wizard Saruman.

SARUMAN THE WHITE
The Saruman minifigure has the same molded beard as Gandalf, but with gray printing. His two variants include one with a printed slope for robes and one with plain white legs.

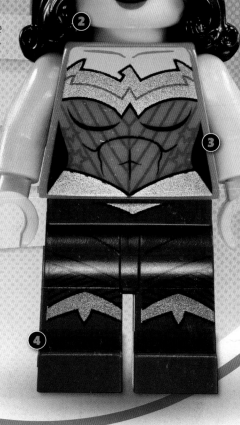

WISH LIST AMAZON!

THE NAME'S PRINCE, DIANA PRINCE!

1 Unique hair piece with silver printing

2 Double-sided head shared with Satele Shan in LEGO® *Star Wars*®

3 Exclusive torso printing continues on reverse

4 2012 variant wears red boots and blue briefs

WONDER WOMAN

MINI STATS

Theme
LEGO® DC Comics™ Super Heroes

Year
2015

First appearance
Gorilla Grodd Goes Bananas (76026)

Rarity

The **2015 variant** of this Amazon princess-turned-super-hero has a new outfit in keeping with her look in the DC Comics "New 52" series. Silver printing replaces the gold seen on her 2012 minifigure, and blue pants cover her previously bare legs.

LOOP DREAMS

The 2012 variant of Wonder Woman comes with her Lasso of Truth. The only other character to carry a lasso is the Cowgirl, included in Minifigures Series 8.

ORDER UP!

SPONGEBOB SQUAREPANTS

1 Indents along edge of head piece give it a sponge-like look

2 Plain yellow torso under "sandwich board" piece

3 Short legs give SpongeBob his square pants

ODD BOBS

11 SpongeBob variants appear in a total of 15 sets.

It's fair to say that all LEGO minifigures have square pants, but not many have a square head! SpongeBob's unique head is a "sandwich board" piece with a LEGO stud on top, over a standard minifigure torso.

HE'S A STAR!

SpongeBob's friend Patrick has his own unique, cone-shaped head, and comes in seven variants including astronaut, pirate, super hero, and just plain old Patrick!

MINI STATS

Theme
LEGO® SpongeBob SquarePants™

Years
2006, 2008

First appearance
The Krusty Crab (3825)

Rarity

MINI STATS

Theme
LEGO® Star Wars®

Year
2007

First appearance
Randomly placed into LEGO Star Wars sets

Rarity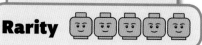

In **2007, 10,000** gold chrome C-3PO minifigures were randomly inserted into LEGO *Star Wars* sets around the world. Shiny enough to satisfy even the fussiest protocol droid, they were made to mark 30 years of *Star Wars*, and came in special bags within each set.

C-3PO (GOLD CHROME)

IN THE SERVICE OF A COLLECTOR, ONE MUST BE PRESENTABLE

1 Gold chrome is plated over ABS plastic elements

2 Same head and printing as original C-3PO minifigure, introduced in 2000.

3 14-carat gold variant has embossed torso, instead of printing

SOLID GOLD
Along with the gold chrome variants, five 14-carat gold C-3POs were also placed inside LEGO *Star Wars* sets in 2007.

UPGRADED
In 2012, the C-3PO minifigure got a new torso print, and printing for his eyes. The 2014 variant adds leg printing for the first time, and even more torso detail.

The DeLorean Time Machine was one of the ideas voted for by fans in the 2012 LEGO Ideas review, and then chosen by the LEGO Group to become an official set. Based on the *Back to the Future* film series, it includes this exclusive minifigure of the movies' time-traveling hero.

1980s MOVIE ICON

IN FLUX
The destination date on the time machine in the set is 28 January 1958—the date the LEGO brick was patented.

GREAT SCOTT!
Marty's friend Doc Brown is also included in the DeLorean set. He shares his hair piece with LEGO® Marvel Super Heroes minifigure Magneto.

MARTY MCFLY

WILL I MEET MY LEGO PARENTS?

1 Same hair piece as Mutt Williams from LEGO® *Indiana Jones*™

2 Reversible head piece with smiling face on one side and a worried expression on the other

3 Exclusive printing on both front and back of torso

4 Same blue pants as Homer in LEGO® *The Simpsons*™ sets

MINI STATS

Theme
LEGO® Ideas

Year
2013

First appearance
DeLorean Time Machine (21103)

Rarity

IT'S SANTA!

LEG-O-HO-HO!

1 Until 2012, all Santa minifigures wore this red hat, more usually seen on LEGO pirates!

2 Long white beard first worn by Majisto the Wizard from the LEGO® Castle theme

3 Black basket with neck bracket has space for a 1x2 LEGO tile

4 In the 2010 LEGO® City Advent Calendar, Santa has bare yellow legs, as he is taking a shower!

SANTA CLAUS

A SLEW OF SANTAS!
Including LEGO® *Star Wars*® variants, there have been 20 different Santa minifigures!

Here's a minifigure you'll really want to find under your Christmas tree! The first in a long line of Santa minifigures, this limited-edition gift-giver came with a sleigh laden with LEGO bricks, and looks just like the real thing!

ADDITIONAL CLAUS
The eighth series of collectible Minifigures includes an all-new Santa Claus with a specially designed hat, sack, and printing. He also appears in Santa's Workshop (set 10245), but with a red sack.

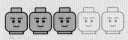

MINI STATS

Theme
LEGO® Town

Year
1995

First appearance
Santa Claus and Sleigh (1807)

Rarity

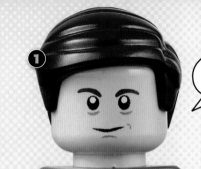

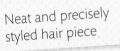
I AM IMMUNE TO YOUR SARCASM!

BAZINGA!

SHELDON COOPER

1 Neat and precisely styled hair piece

2 Famous red T-shirt with "The Flash" logo

3 Red and blue arms depict long-sleeved layered shirt

4 Tan leg piece represents Sheldon's khaki pants

The seven *Big Bang Theory* minifigures were formed in the hot, dense universe of the LEGO Ideas project. The set is the brainchild of LEGO Ideas contributors GlenBricker and Alatariel, and features all of the main characters from the much-loved TV show, each hilariously brought to life in minifigure form.

MINI STATS

Theme
LEGO® Ideas

Year
2015

First appearance
The Big Bang Theory
(21302)

Rarity

FRIENDSHIP ALGORITHM

For their submission, Alatariel and GlenBricker created this design for all seven characters in the set: Leonard, Sheldon, Penny, Howard, Raj, Amy, and Bernadette.

MINI STATS

Theme
LEGO® Star Wars®

Year
2013

First appearance
Duel on Geonosis
(75017)

Rarity

Love this minifigure you will! The original Yoda was the first ever minifigure to sport short legs, and ushered in an era of minifigure children, gnomes, and even Hobbits. This 2013 variant updates the original with a new head mold in a new color, and adds character with printing on the eyes.

SHORT HIS LEGS ARE!

JUDGE ME BY MY SHORT LEGS, DO YOU?

YODA

1 Olive-green head with printed eyes

2 Most Jedi carry a green lightsaber

3 New torso printing has no belt or pouches

4 Short non-posable legs

1

2

3

4

PAST MASTER
The original variant of the Jedi Grand Master came out of exile in 2002. His sand-green head features finely sculpted details, but no printing. He appeared in three sets including Jedi Duel (set 7103).

I'M NOT A MINIFIGURE!

Wondering why one of your favorite LEGO® characters isn't in this book? Then maybe it isn't a minifigure! Most minifigures are made from three standard parts: a head, a torso, and pair of legs; and any LEGO character that doesn't include at least two of those parts doesn't get to call itself a minifigure. Let's meet some of them...

SKELETONS

LEGO® Skeletons rattled onto the scene in 1995. Most have minifigure heads, but a bony handful—such as Samukai from LEGO® NINJAGO™— have special head molds and no standard minifigure parts at all.

DROIDS

In the LEGO® *Star Wars*® universe, droids are the galaxy's go-to robots. Some, like C-3PO, have standard minifigure bodies and special heads, while others including R2-D2 and the battle droids are made entirely from specialized parts.

Created for the LEGO® Friends theme in 2012, mini-dolls also feature in the LEGO® Elves and LEGO® *Disney Princess*™ themes. Just like minifigures, they have separate heads, torsos, and legs, but in more realistic proportions.

MINI-DOLLS

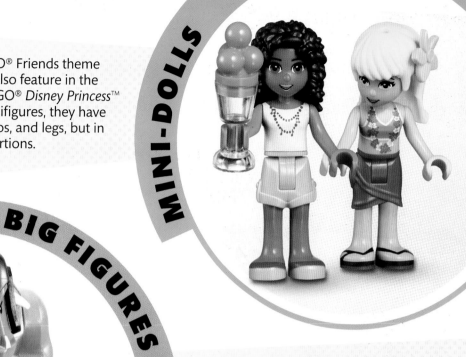

BIG FIGURES

Minifigures have many qualities, but bulk isn't one of them! Big characters need a big figure, and Hagrid from LEGO® Harry Potter™, The Hulk from LEGO® Marvel Super Heroes, and the Giant Troll from LEGO® Castle all stand taller than average.

CREATURES

Though a LEGO monkey does have standard minifigure arms and hands, most LEGO creatures need entirely new elements to look the part. LEGO horses, cows, dogs, and even alligators all have their own special molds.

INDEX

BY CHARACTER NAME

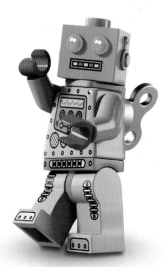

INDEX

Editor Andy Jones
Designer Rhys Thomas
Editorial Assistant Rosie Peet
Additional Designers Thelma-Jane Robb,
Jade Wheaton, Amanda Ghobadi, Gary Hyde
Senior Pre-Production Producer Jennifer Murray
Print Producer Louise Minihane
Managing Editor Simon Hugo
Managing Art Editor Guy Harvey
Art Director Lisa Lanzarini
Publisher Julie Ferris
Publishing Director Simon Beecroft

Writers Jen Anstruther, Jonathan Green, Kate Lloyd, Simon Guerrier
Additional photography Markos Chouris, Gary Ombler

First published in the United States in 2015 by DK Publishing
345 Hudson Street, New York, New York 10014
A Penguin Random House Company

15 16 17 18 19 10 9 8 7 6 5 4 3 2 1
001–259545–Oct/2015

Dorling Kindersley would like to thank: Randi Sørensen, Paul Hansford, Lisbeth Finnemann Skrumsager, Heike Bornhausen, Tara Wike, Chris Bonven Johansen, Tim Ainley, Thomas Ross Parry, Martin Fink, Alexandre Boudon, Adam Corbally, Djordje Djordjevic, Lauge Drewes, and Tore Harmark-Alexandersen at the LEGO Group; Toby Mann, Scarlett O'Hara, Helen Murray, and Tori Kosara for editorial assistance; Lauren Adams, Ellie Bilbow, and Nathan Martin for design assistance.